77-463

FULL EMPLOYMENT, GUIDEPOSTS
AND ECONOMIC STABILITY

*Third in the series of Rational Debate Seminars
sponsored by the American Enterprise Institute
held at
The George Washington University
Washington, D. C.*

FULL EMPLOYMENT, GUIDEPOSTS AND ECONOMIC STABILITY

Arthur F. Burns
Paul A. Samuelson

RATIONAL DEBATE SEMINARS

American Enterprise Institute
for Public Policy Research
Washington, D. C.

Second Printing, 1968

Third Printing, 1971

Library of Congress Catalog Card Number 67-29783

FULL EMPLOYMENT, GUIDEPOSTS AND ECONOMIC STABILITY

Arthur F. Burns
and
Paul A. Samuelson

Published by

American Enterprise Institute
for Public Policy Research

Almost everyone seems to agree with major objectives of U.S. economic policy—full employment, stable prices, and rising productivity. The Employment Act of 1946 sets them down. The President's economic report annually swears its allegiance. The Joint Economic Committee regularly appraises the performance.

But from a day-to-day reading of our newspapers and magazines through the crises of our times, one might easily get the idea that agreement ends with the objectives.

So the American Enterprise Institute invited two eminent economists to discuss how best these objectives could be achieved. One was Dr. Arthur F. Burns, the other Dr. Paul Samuelson. Dr. Burns chaired President Eisenhower's Council of Economic Advisers until 1956, and at the time of the debate in the spring of 1967 was President of the National Bureau of Economic Research. Dr. Samuelson was an adviser to President Kennedy, and is a consultant to the Treasury, the present Council, and the Federal Reserve Board.

What evolved from the lectures, the rebuttals, and the discussion with expert seminar participants was a large area of agreement. This was to be expected, of course, because some part of economics is a science. But despite the acres of common ground, there were critical plots of difference.

Both agreed, for example, that efforts by governments to carry out economic policy have had generally favorable results. They differed on the degree of success. Dr. Burns is inclined to believe that economic policymakers are incapable of doing the right thing at the right time over a sustained period. Dr. Samuelson tends to feel that activists produce better results for the economy than those who are more cautious.

There also were some differences over guideposts, which Dr. Samuelson, as an advocate of the "new economics," was charged with defending. He indicated he thought he might have got the short end of the stick. "For one thing, I am not a wholehearted enthusiast for guideposts; if uncritical enthusiasm were desired, one would have to go elsewhere," he said. Later, he added: "We may with fine rhetoric or telling syllogism slay the presidential guideposts a dozen times; but still, in the opinion of the vast majority of economic experts, we shall be left with the vexing dilemma that free markets do not give us a stable consumers price index at the same time that the rate of unemployment stays down to a socially desirable level." Dr. Samuelson concluded that wage-price guideposts are helpful and have an important role, but are not substitutes for proper macroeconomic fiscal and monetary policies. They are really an attempt to affect the philosophy of men in the marketplace.

Dr. Burns' final comment on guideposts seemed to summarize his opposition: ". . . free markets are our nation's most valuable economic asset, and we should therefore be wary of governmental edicts, perhaps all the more so when they come in the coquettishly modern dress of voluntary guidelines."

Dr. Samuelson attempted to define the difference between "us new economists" and "other economists." "It is our activist attempts to stretch out the prosperity periods by explicit action," he explained.

He recalled the early days of the Kennedy Administration, when he said he was astonished to discover how lawyers in the administration "really believed their own rhetoric—that the country was going to get moving by speaking about getting it moving; and it was a great surprise and required some education for them to realize that you really had to do things to achieve vigorous growth and prosperity."

Nevertheless, many things were done from the beginning. "Expenditures were deliberately expanded," he declared. "There was a great deal of—I hesitate to call it hypocrisy—but of semantic double-talk because there was a great deal of need for the country to adjust itself to rational fiscal thinking. The desire for the investment tax credit by the Kennedy Administration was a genuine desire to stimulate investment by giving revenue, even though, for window-dressing purposes, it was sometimes thought necessary to couple it with revenue-raising verbiage. Eventually too, we had the accelerated depreciation of guidelines of mid-1963. Every time the economy showed signs of lagging, other programs were introduced."

Dr. Burns, however, was not so optimistic about official tinkering over the long haul. Governmental policies dealing with the problems of full employment and economic stability have moved along a rocky road in recent years as in the past, he said. "Since the 1930s, economic policymakers have indeed demonstrated a capacity to learn from past mistakes. Too often, however, their memories have grown dim with the passage of time. Economic generals, like their military counterparts, sometimes forget which war they are fighting, nor do they always know which war to fight. Nevertheless, significant progress has been made, and we must try to extend it."

In his comprehensive review of the economy during the past ten years, Dr. Burns cited a long series of weaknesses in the tools of economics. Among them were limitations on the art of forecasting, incomplete data on job vacancies, inaccurate measurements of prices and costs, and "most important of all, the need to learn better than we yet have the basic truth that, while stability of the general price level will not of itself bring prosperity in the years ahead, we cannot very well maintain international confidence in the dollar or have sustained prosperity without it."

Dr. Burns also criticized "governmental fussing with minor changes in the performance of the economy." These "may easily be ill-timed," he said, "prove ineffective or perverse, and therefore ultimately weaken the effectiveness of governmental policy in handling major problems. We have become too preoccupied with short-run variations of macroeconomic policy, and we do not give enough thought to creating and maintaining an environment that will lessen the burden of discretionary policymaking."

Dr. Samuelson was [1] less concerned about mistakes in economic forecasts, arguing that the activism of the "new economics" usually brings about increases in the money GNP regardless of faulty forecasting. He added that forecasts might even be more inaccurate than sometimes recorded, because the policymakers get "another whack at the control mechanisms," thus achieving their predictions despite the initial misapplication of economic remedies resulting from inaccurate forecasts.

Dr. Burns blamed the "fateful policies of 1965" for the troubles of 1966. Prompt or really good solutions are rarely, if ever, available for imbalances generated by inflation, he argued. He outlined the mistakes of 1965, then asked: "Why did the nation's policymakers, who for years had succeeded so well in monitoring a business expansion under difficult conditions, finally unleash the forces of inflation? Why did men who showed the ability to profit from experience succumb to the oldest weakness of government practice?"

Perhaps these questions are the key to the debate over economic policy. The discussion recorded in this book will not supply final sharp answers; but it may help the reader in his own wisdom decide how much manipulation by policymakers helps, and how much it hurts.

FOREWORD

In this third Rational Debate of the series of four during the 1966-67 academic year, the American Enterprise Institute pursues its most fundamental purpose, to bring before the American public important facts and opinions from which a rational choice can be made between alternative courses in public policy. Rational debate, with the emphasis on "rational," is the keystone of a free society. AEI was founded on this concept in 1943 and continues to operate on it today. Our purpose is to help legislators, policymakers, educators, the press, and the general public to reach informed judgments on major issues of public policy. The Institute conducts research, publishes studies, and sponsors seminars and symposia on these major questions. Statements of the lecturers and other participants in AEI programs are their own, of course; the Institute takes no position on any public policy issue.

The format of AEI's Rational Debates avoids to a great extent the repetition of absolutes in arguing alternatives in public policy and promotes the give and take which can generate rational choices. The choices before us are seldom between the wholly good or the wholly bad. Professor Burns and Professor Samuelson make this abundantly clear in the present volume. The same observation could be made about the other three Rational Debates in the current series, the first between Arthur Schlesinger, Jr., and Alfred de Grazia on *Congress and the Presidency: Their Role in Modern Times;* the second featuring Charles E. Whittaker and William Sloane Coffin, Jr., on *Law, Order and Civil Disobedience;* and the fourth on *The Balance of Payments: Free Versus Fixed Exchange Rates,* with Milton Friedman and Robert V. Roosa.

As I have emphasized in the Forewords to the other Rational Debate books, the American Enterprise Institute hopes that these seminars will contribute to wise policy decisions at all levels of the governments of the United States, federal, state, and local.

September 20, 1967 William J. Baroody
       President
       American Enterprise Institute
        for Public Policy Research

PREFACE

In a year when the economic stability of the nation has
been so widely mooted, the American Enterprise Institute has made an important contribution to the dia-
logue by presenting these two especially distinguished
economists, Professors Arthur F. Burns and Paul A.
Samuelson, in this Rational Debate. They have con-
firmed the suspicions of many that even so complicated
a topic as *Full Employment, Guideposts and Economic
Stability* can be treated lucidly in this relatively short
discourse without slighting any of the fundamentals
involved.

Professors Burns and Samuelson participated in this
three-session debate in April. A select group of government officials, academicians, and newsmen attended.
Many queried the principals in the discussion periods
which followed the formal presentations of lectures and
rebuttals. The general public now has an opportunity
to study the illuminating exchanges.

September 19, 1967

> G. Warren Nutter
> *Coordinator*
> Rational Debate Series

CONTENTS

FIRST LECTURE

ARTHUR F. BURNS

Since the end of World War II, full employment, rising productivity, and a stable price level have been major objectives of economic policy in the United States, as they have in every other industrial country. All segments of our society—businessmen and labor leaders, farmers and urban workers, educators and legislators—now accept and endorse these objectives, particularly the need for full employment. Each year the President's Economic Report reaffirms allegiance to the principles of the Employment Act of 1946. Each year the Joint Economic Committee appraises the President's program for promoting "maximum employment, production, and purchasing power," and prods both the Congress and the executive to pursue whatever measures seem needed to achieve or maintain full employment and economic stability. Each year scores of governmental, business, labor, and civic groups, besides many hundreds of individual economists and other intellectuals, join in the continuing debate on the most appropriate means of achieving the broad economic objectives on which Americans are so generally agreed. The present meeting is one of many such efforts to seek better ways of moving toward our national objectives.

I

The constant attention that we give to public economic policies is proof enough, if any were needed, that the economy rarely performs as well as we think it should. True, we have made considerable progress toward full employment and economic stability in our generation, and we have accomplished this while preserving the essentials of political and economic freedom. Financial crises, which frequently disrupted economic life in earlier times, no longer exacerbate our troubles. Expansions of aggregate economic activity have tended to become longer. Contractions have become both shorter and milder, and the business cycle has lost much of the terror that it held for our fathers. Not only that, but the trend of output per manhour, which is the most vital source of improvement in the general welfare, has moved upward faster than in earlier decades of this century. These gains are impressive when viewed against the background of past experience. However, the yardsticks that we apply to the performance of the economy have also tended to become more exacting, and in any event we have not escaped our share of disappointments. While the level of both employment and production has been generally high and rising during the past 20 years, we have experienced some troublesome recessions. Even in years of extremely brisk activity, such as 1956 and 1966, large groups of people—notably Negroes and teenagers—have continued to be subject to a higher risk of unemployment than the working population at large. And even those workers who have had the good fortune to hold down steady jobs at rising wages have found that their improved money earnings, and also their accumulated savings, are partly illusory on account of the upward tendency of prices.

Economic instability has not yet vanished in our country, any more than it has vanished in any other country that values freedom sufficiently to practice free enterprise on a major scale. Nor, for that matter, has it vanished in the Socialist world where economic life is largely organized on the basis of state edicts. For example, Czechoslovakia experienced a recession in 1963, Communist China suffered a great depression after 1959, Yugoslavia has found it prudent to encourage many of her workers to look for jobs in Western Europe, the Soviet Union has suffered substantial unemployment of the seasonal and frictional type, and Poland has struggled for years with the burden of inefficiency resulting from the practice of requiring its industrial enterprises to absorb more workers than they need. And just as it is impossible to find, whether we look West or East, any final solution to the problem of unemployment, so also it is difficult to find substantial stability of the price level anywhere. Indeed, the advance of the price level of our total output, although it has reduced the purchasing power of the dollar by about 40 percent during the past 20 years, still ranks as one of the better records of the postwar period.

These imperfections of economic achievement, both in

our own past and in other parts of the world, need to be recalled at a time when the course of our economy has again become sluggish. Only two years ago we boasted that the economic expansion which started early in 1961 had already proved more durable than any of its predecessors under peacetime conditions. Now, despite a tremendous upsurge of federal expenditure, which is bound to continue for some time on account of the war in Vietnam, many economists are concerned that our nation may once again be on the brink of recession. Only a short time ago the view was spreading in business and governmental circles that monetary and fiscal policies would henceforth adjust the aggregate demand for goods and services so closely to what the economy can produce at full employment that the danger of recession need no longer be taken seriously. Now, many economists are questioning the skill of governmental policymakers and some are even suggesting that governmental policies have a chronic tendency to destabilize the economy. Any such sweeping generalization can hardly be justified. Nevertheless, in view of recent shifts of fortune and opinion, it may be useful to stop and consider some of the difficulties in the management of prosperity; in particular, how public policy drove the economy forward after 1960, why rapid expansion has temporarily given way to sluggishness, and what guidance can be derived from these experiences for the future. That is my purpose in this evening's lecture.

II

The main source of our national prosperity has always been the hopefulness, initiative, skill, and energy of the American people. By and large, we have also been blessed with good government and with public policies that have left large scope for the expression of these qualities. The increasing attention of government to the problem of full employment and economic stability has led in our generation to ever-changing permutations of policy and they too have left their mark on the character and rate of economic progress. This has been singularly true of the years since 1960 which have been characterized by much boldness and innovation of governmental policy in the economic sphere. History, however, does not divide itself neatly into stages or periods. What happened after 1960 was conditioned by developments in the immediately preceding years.

Taken as a whole, the decade of the 1950s experienced substantial advances in production, employment, and living standards. The later years of the decade, however, brought difficulties in quick succession. The recession following the Korean War came to an early end under the impetus of stimulative governmental policies. But as so often happens in a modern economy, the confidence of the business community soon spilled over into excessive exuberance. During 1956, business construction and the machinery and equipment industries forged ahead at an extremely rapid rate, while the output of the consumer goods trades became sluggish and homebuilding actually slumped. The average level of prices advanced swiftly in wholesale markets, but costs of production rose faster still and profit margins shrank. These and other imbalances gradually undermined the process of expansion. In July, 1957, a recession got under way; and although it proved to be brief, it was the sharpest decline of aggregate activity in the period since World War II. The recovery that followed was strong at the outset, but it soon faltered and it did not return the nation to full prosperity. In the spring of 1960, when the unemployment rate was still 5 percent, the economy again lapsed into recession. During this decline of activity, total output held up exceptionally well. But when the labor force and productivity keep increasing, the mere cessation of growth in physical output suffices to create trouble. Unemployment mounted during 1960 and reached 7 percent in the spring of 1961.

The unsatisfactory performance of the economy in the late 1950s can be blamed in part on governmental timidity or excessive concern over inflation. There were, however, good reasons for concern and caution. The inflation of 1956-57 was fresh in people's memories. President Eisenhower and other high officials realized that the advance of prices would have been smaller if they had moved as promptly and as energetically to curb the excesses of the boom as they had previously moved to check the post-Korean recession. It was only natural that men in authority were resolved not to repeat the mistake. But once the recession started in 1957, the government could not very well remain aloof. Some prominent officials and many private citizens urged a prompt reduction of personal and corporate income tax rates. They pointed out that the nation was still functioning with a tax system that had developed under wartime conditions, and they argued that a lightening of the tax burden would strengthen incentives, enlarge economic horizons, and thereby release fresh and enduring forces of expansion. This compelling plea went unheeded because of fear of budgetary consequences. Instead, credit conditions were eased and federal spending was allowed to expand. The decisions to increase spending did not come at once; they came in a long series, sometimes grudgingly, and thus spread out over months. But when the successive small accretions were finally added up in late 1958, it was discovered that they came to a much larger total than our fiscal authorities had either planned or advocated—indeed, that they made a larger dent in the budget than, say, the $5 billion tax cut that was then being urged would have entailed.

The main impact of the new federal spending programs came after the economy began recovering. A cash deficit of $13 billion, which still stands as the largest annual deficit since 1946, piled up in the fiscal year ending in June, 1959—a year of continuous business expansion. This emergence of a huge deficit at a time of rather rapid economic advance was merely the most dramatic of a series of developments that cast doubt on the financial policy of the government. Over a long stretch of history, it had been characteristic of the level of wholesale prices to fall during contractions of aggregate activity, thereby erasing all or part of the advance that had occurred during the expansion phase. In the recession of 1957-58 wholesale prices departed from rule, actually rose, and thus gave fresh support to the widely held theory that we are living in an age of inflation. This sombre view about the future was reinforced by the deterioration in the balance of payments. During 1958, imports rose sharply, exports fell, and our stocks of gold were cut by two billion dollars. More ominous still, foreign financiers, who hitherto appeared to have unbounded faith in American finances, began to whisper serious doubts whether the integrity of the dollar could be counted on in the future.

Financial developments during 1958 and the fears which they engendered thus strengthened the determination of governmental authorities to try to prevent, now that the economy was again advancing, the sort of excesses that had led to an inflationary boom during 1956-57. Both our international political position and the interests of the domestic economy clearly required better management of prosperity. Having moved too slowly to restrain the preceding expansion, they were ready to move with all necessary speed this time. Still embarrassed by the increase of the discount rate in August, 1957, which came when the boom was already turning into recession, the monetary authorities now took steps to restrain the expansion of credit almost as soon as the first blush of economic recovery was recognized. Before 1958 ended, free reserves of the commercial banks were already wiped out. Pressure on reserves was sharply intensified during 1959. In consequence, the money supply began to decline and interest rates moved up with extraordinary speed. Meanwhile, the budgetary authorities brought the expansion of federal spending to an abrupt halt. Since tax revenues continued to pile up as economic activity grew, the budget moved from an enormous deficit in early 1959 to a sizable surplus 12 months later. Taken together, these fiscal and monetary measures accomplished one of the most violent shifts on record from a policy of stimulation to a policy of restraint.

The abrupt shift of policy proved more restrictive than government officials planned or expected. Largely as a result of their actions, the economic expansion that started in April, 1958, came to a premature end and unemployment rose at a time when it was already excessive. These unhappy consequences, however, had their redeeming side. The very abruptness and magnitude of the policy shift routed an inflationary psychology, demonstrated that ours need not be an age of inflation, forced businessmen to reduce waste and improve efficiency, created sufficient slack in the labor market to impede substantial wage increases, and thus re-established stability in costs and prices. That these conditions were produced without causing a collapse in the state of confidence was an accomplishment of no small significance. The aggregate demand of final buyers, both domestic and foreign, kept growing throughout the recession of 1960-61. Fortunately, the monetary authorities reduced the discount rate one month after the recession started in 1960, instead of raising it one month later as in 1957. The easing of credit helped to maintain aggregate demand and thereby hastened the end of the inventory adjustment. Fiscal policy, in the meantime, remained stubbornly quiescent. Governmental authorities were in no mood to tolerate larger expenditures, nor would they countenance a tax cut which was again being urged by capable and disinterested citizens. In February, 1961, economic expansion resumed and the administration's expectation of an early upturn was vindicated; but before this happened, the nation's electorate decided in a close presidential election to entrust power to the Democratic party.

III

In the course of the campaign of 1960, John F. Kennedy promised that if he were elected president, America would get moving again. He lost no time in giving a new and bolder twist to economic policy. Although his administration can hardly be credited with initiating economic recovery in 1961, it did assume at once a very active role in nursing the recovery and in turning what might have been an ordinary expansion into a remarkable upsurge of the economy. Both political and eco-

nomic circumstances favored an expansionist policy. On
the one hand, the danger of inflation seemed quite re-
mote after three years of stability in average wholesale
prices and in unit costs of production in manufacturing.
On the other hand, the persistence of slack in industrial
capacity and in the labor market created a sense of im-
patience with conservative financial policies. Something
new was expected of the new administration. The merits
of an expansionist fiscal policy—particularly the advan-
tages of a reduction of income taxes over an increase of
governmental expenditures—had been extensively debated since 1957, and the nation was in a mood to try
some fiscal experiments.

In the first year of his administration, President Kennedy chose to move cautiously. By and large, he left it
to his advisers to popularize the teachings of the "new
economics," to give a scholarly dress to the theory of
using fiscal devices to close the gap between actual and
potential output, to create a vision of an economy that
might soon be recession-proof, to demonstrate that the
full-employment surplus (or deficit) is a better index of
the degree of fiscal stimulation than the actual deficit,
to show that the quest for actual budgetary balance
could be self-defeating, and to quiet any lurking fears
of inflation by suggesting guidelines for the proper behavior of prices and wages. The President himself was
more concerned with advancing specific policies for
which the public was prepared—such as speeding of procurement and construction in the interests of recovery,

raising agricultural price supports, liberalizing social security, lifting the minimum wage, extending governmental programs for education, and introducing health insurance for the aged. To be sure, the President did recommend an investment tax credit, but he coupled it with tax increases that would prevent any loss of revenue to the Treasury. He also suggested legislation for stand-by authority under which the President could temporarily reduce individual income tax rates and accelerate spending on public works; but he was much too wise about political matters to expect these measures to win congressional approval in any near future. President Kennedy's caution was plainly reflected in his Budget Message of January, 1962, which called for a small surplus in the next fiscal year.

Even at the outset, however, the budgetary practice of the new administration was less orthodox than the President's rhetoric. Plans for federal spending were repeatedly revised upward during 1961, and actual expenditures followed suit. A surplus in the cash budget of $3.6 billion in 1960 was followed by a deficit of $6.8 billion in 1961—the first of an unbroken series of deficits that is still continuing. Monetary policy also eased and gave strong support to the liberal expenditure policy. As expected, consumer spending responded to these stimuli and so too did investment in inventories. Business investment in plant and equipment failed, however, to develop the vigor that is characteristic of the recovery stage of the business cycle. By the first quarter of 1962, new orders and contracts for plant and equipment were merely 13 percent higher than a year earlier, in contrast to increases of 86 percent, 43 percent, and 31 percent during the corresponding stage of the three preceding expansions. Unemployment diminished, but its rate of decline was abnormally slow. Evidently, the recovery was not proceeding as well as had been hoped, despite the large fiscal and monetary stimuli.

The weak link in the chain of economic recovery was business investment in fixed capital. In popular discussions, this was generally attributed to the existence of excess industrial capacity. However, a good deal of idle capacity always develops in the course of a business slump, and yet this condition has never been a bar to brisk expansion of investment once confidence recovers. New firms are then established in larger numbers; existing firms in turn speed investments associated with innovation; firms that have done well despite the slump enlarge their capacity in anticipation of stronger markets; while many of the firms that have fallen behind in the competitive race finally embark on substantial programs of modernization. If these responses were not strongly felt in 1961, the reason was a want of sufficient confidence. Overinvestment in 1956-57, the steadily rising trend of wages, the tendency of profit margins to shrink during the past dozen years, the sharply reduced rate of economic growth during the past three or four years— all these factors contributed to business caution, and so too did the coming of a new administration whose economic policies could not as yet be fairly assessed. Many businessmen were concerned that trade unions, which had contributed to the victory of the Democratic party at the polls, would soon become bolder in their demands for higher wages and larger fringe benefits. Some feared that larger governmental spending, however favorable to markets in the short run, would in due course be followed by higher taxes. Others feared that direct controls of prices might eventually be undertaken by the government in order to check the inflationary pressures that would result from its fiscal and monetary policies, and still others were concerned on all these grounds.

The uneasiness of the business community reached a climax in April, 1962, when President Kennedy moved sternly to force the steel companies to rescind the price increase that they had just posted. This action by the President had no clear sanction in law and it caused consternation in business circles. Men reasoned that if the government could coerce or punish the steel industry today, it might move next against the automobile industry or the aluminum industry or any other. Since the beginning of 1962 economic recovery had shown some signs of hesitation. Now, with confidence shaken and a large inventory adjustment in the steel industry unavoidable, the continuance of business expansion became more doubtful. The stock market reflected the mood of the time by experiencing its sharpest break of the entire postwar period. Orders for machinery and equipment were cut back here and there. Private borrowing stopped rising, raw materials prices softened, profit margins narrowed, and unemployment stopped declining. The curve of industrial production, which had risen smartly until April, 1962, flattened out for the rest of the year.

Fortunately, an imminent recession was forestalled. Recognizing that the government's handling of the steel price problem had disturbed the business community, President Kennedy turned at once to the difficult task of rebuilding confidence. In one address after another, he and his lieutenants now stressed the dependence of our national prosperity on free markets, higher profits, and larger investment in fixed capital. These reassurances were soon followed by measures to reduce the tax burden borne by the business community. In July, 1962, the Treasury announced that business firms could henceforth reckon their income taxes on the basis of shorter and more realistic estimates of the life of depreciable facilities. This basic tax reform was long overdue and it was welcomed by businessmen. With the President's prodding, the Congress enacted later in the year an investment tax credit which had already been proposed in 1961, but which was now substantially modified to make it more acceptable to the business community.

In the late summer of 1962 the President made his boldest move. His studies of the tax policies of other countries had convinced him that our tax system was a heavy drag on enterprise and investment. In view of the slowdown of the economy, a "quick" temporary tax cut had its appeal, but the Ways and Means Committee of the House of Representatives was more interested in permanent reform and legislation of this character could not be adopted quickly. In the circumstances, the President concluded that the time was right to announce his intention to request the Congress at the beginning of the next session to adopt a sweeping reform of the income tax, the main thrust of which would be a massive reduction of tax rates for corporations and for individuals in every income bracket. This tax proposal marked a radical departure in economic policymaking. In 1958 and again in 1960, when the country was experiencing recession, a tax cut had been repeatedly urged as a recovery measure that promised prompt results. Now, the purpose was to remove the fiscal drag on an expansion which was still under way, to extend thereby the advance of prosperity, and to risk fiscal deficits for an indefinite period to realize this objective.

The new tax policies and the new tone of governmental pronouncements had the desired effect on business and investor sentiment. Fears of hostile governmental intervention in the day-by-day activities of business firms subsided. Although many businessmen did not like the budgetary implications of a massive tax cut at a time when a deficit was already in the making, they also were quick to see that stimulation of the economy through tax reduction would serve to strengthen the private sector of the economy. In any event, the policy of favoring investment was a significant departure from the traditional policy of the Democratic party, and this fact was not lost on the business community. With optimism reviving and the state of inventories in better shape, economic conditions in late 1962 were ripe for a new wave of expansion. By the end of the year, business commitments for investment in fixed capital began rising again, and fears of an early recession soon vanished.

In all, about a year and a half elapsed between President Kennedy's announcement of his plan for tax reduction and its actual enactment. There were two major reasons for the long delay. First, the President's fiscal program, as presented to the Congress early in 1963, called for numerous revisions in the tax laws as well as a general tax reduction; and while the latter was welcomed widely, the former evoked powerful opposition. Second, the President projected an increase of budget expenditures of $4.5 billion for the next fiscal year besides a net tax reduction of over $10 billion. Many influential citizens who supported a reduction of taxes were sharply opposed to a simultaneous increase of expenditure on the ground that such a fiscal policy would entail a protracted series of deficits. The fate of the President's program therefore seemed very uncertain for a time. But as the issues surrounding the program were debated within and outside the halls of Congress, it became increasingly apparent that the President's main objective was the tax reduction, and that he would yield ground to his opponents on other parts of the fiscal package. More and more citizens therefore came to feel that they would not need to wait much longer for a reduction in taxes. Finally, in March, 1964, when Lyndon Johnson was already carrying the burdens of the presidency, the tax cut became law. But months before that, the growing expectation of its adoption stimulated individuals and business firms to plan and spend more daringly. The expansion of economic activity, which was gradually cumulating of its own momentum, thus moved ahead on a wave of increasing confidence. The gross national product, expressed in real terms, rose 4 percent between 1962 and 1963 and well over 5 percent between 1963 and 1964.

IV

By early 1964, the expansion of economic activity had already lasted longer than the average duration of a business-cycle expansion. Nevertheless, the economy gave every indication that the advance would continue. Throughout 1964, as production and employment continued to rise, the structure of economic activity remained well balanced. A much faster pace in the output of business capital goods than in the output of consumer goods was only beginning. The ratio of inventories to sales in major branches of production and trade remained low or moved still lower. The wholesale price level was substantially steady. Although consumer prices kept rising, the advance was gentle. Although wages kept increasing, they advanced at nearly the same rate as the overall improvement in productivity, so that unit costs of production remained quite stable. Profits grew with the volume of business, besides benefiting from revisions in the tax laws—among them, a reduction of income tax rates which became effective during the year. Stock prices moved up, but no faster than corporate earnings. With prices in our wholesale markets steady, while much of the rest of the world practiced inflation, exports rose sharply and a larger surplus on merchandise trade piled up than in any year since 1947. Meanwhile, interest rates remained fairly steady. In view of the still precarious state of the balance of payments, the monetary authorities sanctioned a moderate rise of short-term market rates of interest; but the interest rates of largest significance to businessmen—customer rates on bank loans, bond yields, and mortgage yields—remained at or below the level reached at the bottom of the recession in 1961.

Moreover, while federal revenues in 1964 continued to fall short of expenditures, the deficit now reflected lower tax rates rather than any further increase of spending. In the debates that preceded the Revenue Act of 1964, some citizens had urged larger federal spending as the best way to stimulate the economy, others argued for tax reduction, and still others felt that it would be well to travel both roads at the same time. President Kennedy was favorably inclined to the mixed approach, but he put much the heavier emphasis on tax reduction. Even so, the Congress balked. The preamble to the House bill explicitly assigned top fiscal priority to tax reduction, with debt reduction next. This meant, as Congressman Wilbur Mills explained to the House, that the nation was choosing tax reduction, and rejecting larger spending, as its "road to a bigger, more progressive economy." In order to assure adoption of the tax cut, President Kennedy assented to the preamble and President Johnson did likewise a little later. Indeed, in his first Budget Message, presented in January, 1964, President Johnson called for smaller expenditures under the administrative budget in fiscal 1965 than in fiscal 1964. With this much assured, the Senate promptly passed the House bill with only minor revisions. And in line with the new fiscal policy, federal spending actually stopped rising for a time. From the third quarter of 1963 to the first quarter of 1965, cash expenditures remained virtually constant. Thus, private enterprise and private demand once again became the great energizing force of the economy.

At the end of 1964, economic activity had already been advancing for almost four years. The expansion was proving remarkably durable, but it was not yet exceptionally rapid or intense. This very fact, no less than the deliberate economic planning of the time, contributed to the prolongation of the advance. If the investment in plant and equipment was sluggish at the start, this facilitated more vigorous activity later. If the investment in fixed capital and in inventories was checked in 1962, that too contributed to greater activity later. If the shift toward public policies that were more mindful of business interests took place gradually, that in its turn helped to keep business optimism within moderate bounds. The expansion was thus the product of many causes, and not the least among them was the inheritance of price and cost stability. As late as 1964 there was still a fair amount of slack in the economy, and this condition continued to exercise a restraining influence on the market behavior of both businessmen and labor leaders. The fact, moreover, that productivity improved somewhat faster after 1960 than in the preceding quinquennium made it easier for business firms to pay higher wages without incurring higher costs per unit of output. In the environment of rough stability of costs and prices that ruled until 1964, there was little reason to accumulate inventories as a hedge against inflation. Nor was there any need to rush investments in fixed capital on the ground that costs were likely to be appreciably higher next year than now.

Thus, our economy in 1964 had the qualities of order and balance, besides considerable momentum from within the private sector. To be sure, signs were not lacking that the vigor of expansion was rapidly reducing the slack in productive capacity. Prices of sensitive raw materials had begun rising in spirited fashion as early as the fall of 1963. By the late summer of 1964 a significant increase had already occurred in the number of business firms reporting slower deliveries of merchandise. In the closing months of 1964, price increases in wholesale markets—while usually quite small—had become rather widespread. Toward the end of 1964 the unemployment rate for married men—who constitute, of course, the more skilled and experienced part of the labor force—

had dropped to the level that ruled during the boom of
1956-57. By the end of the year, the length of the average workweek in manufacturing was already at the
level reached during the Korean War. However, in the
exhilarating economic and political atmosphere that
ruled in the closing months of 1964, it was easy to overlook these and other indications of increasing pressure
on the nation's available resources.

V

Clearly, no small part of the economic improvement
was due to the government's tax policy combined with
monetary ease. With the unemployment rate still close
to 5 percent at the beginning of 1965, it seemed only
fitting and proper to the managers of our national prosperity to press harder the general policy of economic
stimulation that had proved so dramatically successful.
The second installment of the income tax reduction for
corporations and individuals became effective in January, but that was deemed insufficient. The President
urged in addition a reduction of excise taxes, and this
proposal evoked such enthusiasm in the Congress that
only 34 days elapsed between the introduction of the
excise bill and the President's signature. The new law
aimed to reduce excises by $2.2 billion in the fiscal year
beginning July, 1965, and by nearly $5 billion on a full-
year basis when all the reductions would take effect.
These tax reductions were not yet the whole of the fiscal
stimulus applied in 1965. With the war in Vietnam in-

tensifying and new civilian programs clamoring for governmental favor, the fiscal philosophy enunciated in the preamble of the Revenue Act of 1964 was quickly forgotten. By the last quarter of 1965, the annual rate of federal cash expenditure was already $12 billion higher than in the first quarter.

These fiscal expedients imparted, of course, a fresh stimulus to economic expansion. Since the economy was now booming, governmental revenues rose despite the new tax reductions. Nevertheless, the deficit increased during 1965, and this need for finance was reinforced by a tremendous upsurge of borrowing by business firms and consumers. On their part, the monetary authorities made sure that the growing demands for credit would be met. In fact, they supplied the commercial banks with reserves so generously that the banks were able to add to their investments in securities, besides adding abundantly to their loans. Indebtedness to commercial banks rose by $25 billion during 1965, in contrast to $16 billion during 1963 and $18 billion during 1964. Total debt, both public and private, grew by $96 billion during 1965, in contrast to about $77 billion during each of the two preceding years. With credit expanding all around, the money supply could not stand still. The nation's stock of money, which had grown at an average annual rate of less than 3 percent between mid-1960 and mid-1964, rose at a rate of over 4 percent between June, 1964, and April, 1965, and at a rate of nearly 6 percent the rest of 1965. Thus, as the economy approached full employment, monetary policy became increasingly expansionist. And so, too, did fiscal policy. The full-employment surplus, which had become the official measure of fiscal stimulus, moved irregularly between 1961 and 1963, fell in 1964, and was nearly wiped out by the end of 1965.

The accelerating use of monetary and fiscal stimuli served to narrow very quickly the remaining gap, as the Council of Economic Advisers reckoned it, between the nation's actual and potential output. As 1965 drew to a close, the nation could rejoice that the unemployment rate was finally down to 4 percent—the level which the Council had previously adopted as a reasonable target for full utilization of resources. But the widespread upsurge of public and private spending produced also other and less welcome results—in wholesale markets, prices that were 4 percent higher than in mid-1964; in consumer markets, prices that were nearly 3 percent higher; in the labor market, wages that were beginning to rise at an increasing rate; and in the money and capital market, interest rates that were moving up sharply, despite an enormous expansion in the supply of credit. These evidences of strain on the economy's resources became stronger during 1966. By the fall of the year, wholesale prices rose another 2.5 percent, consumer prices over 3.5 percent, while interest rates reached their highest level in about 40 years.

Worse still, the economy became seriously distorted by 1966. In the first place, as bottlenecks on the supply side became widespread, the hectic advance of physical production could not continue. Crosscurrents in the economy therefore multiplied and the high expectations of many businessmen were frustrated. Second, a large gap between the rate of growth of business investment in fixed capital and the rate of growth of consumer spending had already lasted three years, and this imbalance in the structure of production could also not long continue. Third, concern over possible shortages and slow deliveries caused inventories to rise faster than sales in the early months of 1966. Later in the year, as the growth of sales weakened, inventories began to pile up involuntarily. Fourth, profits became vulnerable as a result of the divergent movements of prices and wages. The advance of wholesale prices abated after mid-1966, mainly because of weakness in farm and industrial materials prices, while the rise of consumer prices quickened. With profits high, the demand for labor strong, and the consumer price level rising at a disconcerting rate, the upward push of wages accelerated. Meanwhile, numerous factors slowed down the advance of productivity—among them, the poorer quality of newly hired labor, more rapid labor turnover, lesser diligence of employees, accumulating fatigue of workers and their managers, slower and less dependable delivery of materials and equipment, the need to keep much high-cost equipment in use, and the need here and there to bring obsolete equipment back into use. The net result was that the rate of increase of output per manhour not only slackened, but fell below the rate of increase of wages per hour. With demand pressures, particularly in the consumer sector, beginning to wane, while unit labor costs were rising all around, a cost-price squeeze developed in the world of business.

These forces internal to the boom, which were now causing readjustments in the economy, were heavily influenced, but in conflicting directions, by governmental policy. Federal cash expenditures moved up with extraordinary rapidity, and reached an annual rate of $156 billion in the second half of 1966, in contrast to a rate of $130 billion a year earlier. Tax revenues also rose rapidly in 1966, largely but by no means entirely as a result of the boom. Higher social security taxes that had previously been legislated went into effect at the beginning of the year. A little later, some excises were raised and a speedup of tax payments was ordered. In the fall the investment tax credit was suspended. Nevertheless, as estimates of the full-employment surplus indicate, fiscal policy taken as a whole became even more expansionist in 1966 than in 1965.

But if fiscal policy was still highly stimulative, monetary policy became severely restrictive. As signs of inflation multiplied in 1965, the monetary authorities became concerned that their policy of active credit ease was being carried too far. They were troubled by the deterioration in the basic condition of the balance of payments as well as by domestic developments. As characteristically happens during a boom, imports were now rising much more swiftly than exports. Besides, the war in

Vietnam was causing large and increasing foreign exchange costs. In December, 1965, the monetary authorities finally overcame their hesitation and raised the discount rate, despite strong opposition from the White House; but they continued for another few months to allow bank credit to grow at practically the same rate as before. By the spring of 1966, when it became apparent that the stimulative thrust of fiscal policy was not abating, they shifted bluntly to a policy of credit restriction, thus repeating a familiar pattern. Many businesses, even large and well established corporations, that sought to borrow from their commercial banks, now discovered that they would have to get along with less credit or try to find credit elsewhere. But other financial institutions—life insurance companies, mutual savings banks, and particularly the savings and loan associations —could not extend significant relief, since they were even more hard pressed than the commercial banks. In this constricted environment of finance, not only did interest rates move up rapidly from a level that was already abnormally high, but the public market for debt instruments became disorganized for a while, and total private borrowing in the final quarter fell to the lowest level for that season since 1962.

The credit squeeze reinforced the gathering forces of readjustment in the economy. The homebuilding industry, which is peculiarly dependent on credit, became the outstanding casualty of financial stringency. Many real estate firms and small businesses in other lines of activity were injured. Moreover, the high interest rates brought depression to the bond market, and became a major negative influence on the stock market as well. Tight money, however, was not the only factor now disciplining the boom. With the scope of economic expansion narrowing, labor costs rising, profit margins shrinking, construction costs running well above investors' estimates, uncertainty about the course of federal finances growing, and the business mood gradually becoming less exuberant, powerful forces besides tight money operated to bring the investment boom to a close. Consumer markets also lost their vigor as many families began practicing stricter economies in order to cope with the rising cost of living. In the meantime, inventories soared and the need to bring them into closer relation to sales cast a cloud on the economic outlook for the months immediately ahead.

VI

The recent sluggishness of the economy has inevitably led to much questioning of governmental policy. In particular, the monetary authorities have been blamed for bringing on a damaging credit shortage and unacceptably high interest rates last year. The critics are undoubtedly right if they mean that the shift from easy to tight money need not have been so blunt. But the complaint of some goes deeper; namely, that the government should have seen to it that interest rates remained at the moderate level that ruled until mid-1965. It is doubtful whether such a result could have been achieved. If the monetary authorities had attempted to peg interest rates, the boom would have become still more intense and the demand for credit would have risen still faster. The resulting open inflation, quite apart from other grave consequences, could have made interest rates rise eventually even more than they did. After all, when the price level is going up fast and constantly, lenders will in the end seek to be compensated for the depreciation of money during the period of the loan, and no central bank can force lenders to do anything else. As it was, the advance of interest rates before April, 1966, merely reflected the fact that the demand for credit had become so intense that it rose even faster than the extraordinary rise in the supply of credit. It was only then that the authorities stepped bluntly on the credit brake.

The fiscal authorities also have not escaped criticism. In view of the scale of federal spending and the escalation of the war in Vietnam, they have been repeatedly blamed for not raising income tax rates early in 1966. It seems likely that if defense costs had not been greatly underestimated, income taxes would actually have gone up. In that event, monetary policy would probably have been less restrictive, the homebuilding industry would have fared better, and some of the gyrations in financial markets would have been avoided. On the other hand, since retail trade was already beginning to display some signs of sluggishness, higher income taxes on individuals might well have accentuated the slackening rate of expansion. The case was perhaps stronger for a temporary increase in the corporate income tax or a suspension of the investment tax credit; but any such measure would also have come at an inconvenient time—that is, when profit margins were already beginning to recede. As things happened, the suspension of the investment tax credit did not become law until November, the very month when the Federal Reserve authorities had already begun relaxing the credit restraints.

The fact is that prompt or really good solutions are rarely, if ever, available for the imbalances generated by inflation. Once forces of inflation have been released, it becomes very difficult to bring them under control without some sizable readjustments in the economy. Mistakes in economic policy were undoubtedly made in 1966 as in every year; but they largely derived from the fateful policies of 1965 when, despite the larger spending on defense, practically every weapon in the arsenal of economic stimulation was brought into use—greater monetary ease, lower income tax rates for individuals, lower income tax rates for corporations, lower excise taxes, and larger spending on programs of the Great Society. All this happened when moderate measures of restraint rather than accelerated stimuli were needed, so that the expanding economy could retain its balance. And so we finally come to the agonizing question: why did the nation's policymakers, who for years had succeeded so well in monitoring a business expansion under difficult conditions, finally unleash the forces of inflation? Why did men who showed the ability to profit from experience succumb to one of the oldest weaknesses of governmental practice?

One reason, I think, is that they were misled by the very success that for a time attended their efforts. Economic expansion was continuing, and the level of costs and prices was remaining steady. Even the disequilibrium in the balance of payments no longer seemed so formidable. The export surplus had risen steadily since 1962 and, disagreeable though it would be to do so, the adverse capital movement could be handled by special measures —such as the interest equalization tax of 1963 or new guidelines for foreign loans and investments. With production, employment, personal incomes, and corporate profits going up steadily, and the consumer price level rising less rapidly than in earlier years, the nation's electorate returned the administration to power with an overwhelming vote of confidence in November, 1964. Economic policies for and during 1965 were shaped in this atmosphere of success, to which the Council of Economic Advisers had made a very notable contribution. The massive tax cut was its bold conception, and the enactment of such a measure at a time when the economy was advancing smoothly was a triumph of the "new economics."

The central doctrine of this school is that the stage of the business cycle has little relevance to sound economic policy; that policy should be growth-oriented instead of cycle-oriented; that the vital matter is whether a gap exists between actual and potential output; that fiscal deficits and monetary tools need to be used to promote expansion when a gap exists; and that the stimuli should be sufficient to close the gap—provided significant inflationary pressures are not whipped up in the process. The magnitude of the stimulus to be applied in any particular case involves, of course, difficult estimating and forecasting, but the Council's forecasts were apparently improving. Its economic forecast for 1962 was wide of the mark; it was better for 1963 and it was nearly perfect for 1964. In judging economic prospects for 1965, the diminished slack in the economy could not be ignored. But if the margin for expansionist policies appeared smaller on this account, the guidelines for prices and wages could increase it. That, indeed, was their basic purpose. Originally presented as a contribution to public discussion, they had by now been shaped into crisp rules that might lead to censure of violators or worse. With the price level nearly steady and unemployment still well above 4 percent, it thus seemed tolerably safe as well as desirable to resort to fiscal and monetary stimuli on a larger scale than before. But as later experience demonstrated, neither trade unions nor business firms will act often or long in a manner that is contrary to their economic interests. Once slack in the economy was significantly reduced, expectations of stable prices began to fade, inflationary pressures reappeared, and their initial symptoms were already visible in 1964, as I previously noted.

The policymakers paid slight attention to these cyclical symptoms, for their thinking was focused on bringing down the rate of unemployment—an objective to which the government was rightly committed. An unemployment rate of 4 percent, or possibly somewhat less, had always been the objective of the administrators of the Employment Act. But in 1961 the figure of 4 percent became official for the first time, and this inevitably added to public pressure for its prompt realization. However, the economic significance of any particular figure of unemployment does not stay fixed in a dynamic environment. In recent times, the labor market has changed profoundly as the numbers working part-time or intermittently grew relative to the stable full-time labor force, as voluntary unemployment became a larger factor in the total, and as job opportunities for the unskilled declined. These structural changes in the labor market tended to make it harder to reach an unemployment rate of 4 percent merely by stimulating aggregate demand. But if this was the case, it was desirable by 1965 to shift the emphasis of economic policy from expanding aggregate demand to the correction of structural maladjustments. The administration read the evidence differently, and it did so in part because of the theoretical apparatus of the Council of Economic Advisers. Since the Council identified an unemployment rate of 4 percent with a condition of practically full employment, this figure served as a constant in the equation for computing the potential output. The gap between actual and potential output, in turn, was attributed to a defi-

ciency of aggregate demand; so that, in effect, any unemployment in excess of 4 percent called for correction
of an alleged demand shortage. This was a dangerous
shortcut in analysis, since the gap could obviously arise,
in whole or in part, from obstacles on the side of supply
or from a failure of the constituent parts of demand and
supply to adjust sufficiently to one another. To analyze
the labor market on these principles, the Council would
have needed comprehensive statistics on job vacancies.
Unfortunately, such statistics did not—and still do not
—exist.

Faulty statistics compounded the difficulties of the
policymakers. When industrial markets tighten, list
prices for a time are apt to remain unchanged, while
effective prices are raised by reducing special concessions
or charging a premium. Since these common departures
from list prices are largely ignored in the official index
of wholesale prices, the rise that it registered in 1964
and 1965 undoubtedly understated the actual rise. Another statistical deficiency was still more mischievous.
As originally calculated by the Department of Commerce, the annual rate of increase in the gross national
product during 1965 was consistently too low, quarter
after quarter, by amounts varying from about $2 to $5
billion. This cumulation of errors left its mark on economic thinking by underestimating the growth that was
taking place, and therefore also exaggerating whatever
gap may have still existed between actual and potential
output.

Thus, the psychology of success, the novel guidelines for prices and wages, technical economic analysis, and its statistical accoutrements, all played their role in moving the nation to a more expansionist economic policy during 1965. But the role of philosophic views and political factors, which are always and inevitably present, may well have exceeded everything else. The main drive for an expansionist policy came from the executive establishment. The Congress generally acquiesced, and so too for a while did the Federal Reserve Board which still had some misgivings about the degree of caution that it had exercised in the past. Nowadays, the view is widely held in economic and political circles that a little inflation is tolerable because it can lead to a reduction of unemployment and some alleviation of poverty. The longer-run relations of inflation, unemployment, and poverty are less well understood. Thus, with prosperity increasing, it seemed only proper to the President and his advisers to take bolder steps in behalf of the sectors of the economy that had been left behind by the march of progress. With income taxes already lowered, it seemed only just to reduce excises and thus aid both merchant and consumer, whether rich or poor. The growing involvement in Vietnam came gradually and it was not expected to be a major factor financially. As the year advanced, it became evident even to many of those who supported the guidelines policy that trade unions and business corporations either would not or could not discharge adequately the responsibility of hold-

ing back the tide of inflation which the government, in
effect, had asked them to assume. Indeed, by mid-1965,
the Federal Reserve authorities had already become
gravely concerned about the course of events; but they
were reluctant to take immediate measures that would
run counter to the policy of the executive—the main
source of governmental power. Time is always needed to
carry out a significant shift of policy by a far-flung government of divided powers, particularly when the move
requires restraints on expansion. In this instance, the
difficulty was magnified by the political cost of returning
to orthodox policies for fighting inflation.

Theories have a power that administrators, no matter
how able, cannot fully control. By and large, economic
policy during 1965 was still governed by the theory that
stimulation of activity was reasonably safe as long as
a gap existed between actual and potential output, no
matter how small the gap was becoming or how rapidly
it was being closed. When small inflationary signs appeared, they were at first not believed or dismissed as
trivial. By the time a change in policy was attempted,
it had already been pushed into greater stimulation than
was intended. Thus, deliberately expansionist measures
were carried along passively for a time as the desirability
of a shift in policy and how it might best be executed
were being pondered by the managers of our prosperity.

VII

The course of economic policy in the United States in

recent years, despite some disturbing misadventures, remains impressive. Since 1960 we surely have made progress in moving toward our national objectives. Production and employment rose substantially, the advance of prosperity became widely diffused, full employment was re-established, and new doors of economic opportunity were opened up to underprivileged citizens. The government played a vital part in bringing about these gains by its imaginative, and yet pragmatic, approach to the nation's problems. When increases of federal spending failed to produce desired results, it shifted boldly to tax reduction, and thus made the psychology of confidence its ally in the quest for economic improvement. When structural maladjustments in the labor market became clearer, it proceeded to build on the modest beginnings of the Manpower Development and Training Act. And when inflation broke loose, it finally recognized that orthodox financial measures were better suited to our nation's genius than legal props for the badly bruised wage and price guidelines.

However, this willingness to learn from experience came much too slowly at times, and in any event recent years have brought disappointments as well as successes. Certainly, extensive unemployment lasted much too long, the disequilibrium in the balance of payments escaped correction, the federal government continued to run a deficit even when full employment was re-established, the nation experienced another round of inflation and this, together with the large fluctuations in financial markets, resulted in a redistribution of wealth that injured many defenseless citizens. Economic policy cannot escape a part of the responsibility for these failures, some of which may yet haunt us in the future.

Thus, governmental policies for dealing with the problem of full employment and economic stability have moved along a rocky road in recent years as in the past. Since the 1930s, economic policymakers have indeed demonstrated a capacity to learn from past mistakes. Too often, however, their memories have grown dim with the passage of time. Economic generals, not unlike their military counterparts, sometimes forget which war they are fighting, nor do they always know which war to fight. Nevertheless, significant progress has been made and we must try to extend it.

The needs are many, and so too are the opportunities. We need to become better aware of the limitations of the art of economic forecasting even as we try to improve it. We need to develop comprehensive data on job vacancies, so that it will no longer be necessary to guess whether or when a deficiency in aggregate demand exists. We need to improve our measures of prices and costs, so that inflationary pressures can be recognized more promptly. We need to develop quarterly projections of federal revenues and expenditures, similar to the information now compiled by the government on business sales expectations and investment intentions, so that the changing requirements of fiscal policy can be better evaluated than in the past or at present. We need to learn more about the subtle forces that shape the state of confidence. We need to develop policies for dealing with seasonal unemployment—a problem that we have largely ignored since the 1920s. We need to concentrate more heavily on labor market policies, including a reform of the minimum wage, so that we will be less tempted to seek through expansionist policies what can be achieved at lower cost and with more lasting effect by attending to structural causes of unemployment. We need to strengthen the existing automatic stabilizers and try to devise sensible new ones, so that the burdens of discretionary policy may be somewhat lighter. We need to learn to act, at a time when the economy is threatened by inflation, with something of the sense of urgency that we have so well developed in dealing with the threat of recession. We need to learn to make necessary shifts of economic policy more promptly, so that they may be gradual instead of abrupt. And most important of all, we need to learn better than we yet have the basic truth that, while stability of the general price level will not of itself bring prosperity in the years ahead, we cannot very well maintain international confidence in the dollar or have sustained prosperity without it.

SECOND LECTURE

PAUL A. SAMUELSON [1]

I realize that this is a debate whose title might crudely be put—"Resolved: Wage-Price Guideposts are Obnoxious, Harmful if Effective but Inevitably Ineffective." Professor Burns is the speaker for the affirmative, and I have the not completely enviable task of being speaker for the negative.

It reminds me of a debate I engaged in during the war. It appeared in a businessman's magazine and had as its title—"Resolved: Easy Money is a Bad Thing for the Country." The public-spirited banker Hans Christian Sonne upheld the affirmative, and I had to develop the case for easy money. As was the custom, readers were polled to see who had won the debate. When the final score was counted, I was behind 75 percent to 25 percent; but the kind editor wrote me saying that, before his audience and on such a subject, I had done so well that I was to be congratulated.

Actually, I propose to treat this as a seminar, adhering literally to the title of this series. For one thing I am not a wholehearted enthusiast for guideposts; if uncritical enthusiasm were desired, one would have to go elsewhere. Many aspects of guideposts I do admire, but at points I shall have to be the devil's advocate in an adversary procedure designed to bring out truth and balance.

One final note of introduction. My title is "Wage-Price Guideposts and the Need for Informal Controls in a Mixed Economy." The words are selected so that our discussion can fruitfully go beyond the wage and price issues raised by Kennedy-Johnson doctrines to the more general issues that confront the American economy.

Are informal controls over bank lending abroad a good or bad thing: What about the so-called voluntary program by American corporations to limit direct foreign investments which worsen our balance of payments?

Many of the same issues, philosophical and technical, are raised by this problem as by that of the guideposts.

What are we to think of the familiar Federal Reserve weapon called "moral suasion"? Only last year the Federal Reserve went out of its way to issue a formal letter cautioning banks against excessive lending, but assuring them that banks which perform in the public interest would receive favorable treatment at the discount window. And, of course, earlier this year when the economy proved to be turning soft, the Federal Reserve ostentatiously issued a letter revoking the previous letter of restraint.

Although my examples are current and American, these are lasting issues for debate in every modern mixed economy. The Dutch do not have a President, but the Netherlands government has been struggling for a decade with the problem of "an incomes policy." France does have a strong head of state and a plan, but it too must try to reconcile the dilemma of full employment and price stability. Before this audience I don't suppose I have to add to the praises of the West German miracle. Close study of that experience shows that the West German Republic is a far cry from a laissez-faire economy. At the same time that Ludwig Erhard was writing fine words about the free market, he was turning on the spigot of residential construction by *ad hoc* tax concessions; and whenever this or that export trade showed signs of flagging, some new measure was cooked up in Bonn that would have been the admiration of Sidney Webb and the despair of Frederick Bastiat or Friedrich Hayek. But my point in this connection is that the German economy, like every present-day mixed economy, is still far from approaching a solution to the problem of creeping inflation.

We may with fine rhetoric or telling syllogism slay the presidential guideposts a dozen times; but still, in the opinion of the vast majority of economic experts, we shall be left with the vexing dilemma that free markets do not give us a stable consumers price index at the same time that the rate of unemployment stays down to a socially desirable minimum.

BACKGROUND OF GUIDEPOSTS

During the great slump of the 1930s economists learned that expansionary fiscal and monetary policies could bring a depressed economic system toward full employment. You might call these the days of happy and simple Keynesianism.

However, by the end of World War II when full employment had long been a reality, the honeymoon was over. The issue of price instability at full employment stared economists in the face. I suppose the famous Beveridge Report of the mid-1940s in England was the first to state forcefully this dilemma. (Parenthetically, our own Employment Act of 1946 tactfully avoided noticing the problem.)

Then there was a dramatic series of unsigned articles in the *Economist* predictive that ours would be an age of inflation. These articles asked the question:

Can any modern mixed economy simultaneously enjoy
  1) full employment
  2) stability of the general price index
  3) free commodity and collective bargaining markets uncontrolled by government fiats?

The author, who I believe was Peter Wiles, then a young scholar at Oxford, answered his own question in the negative. Either you must give up full employment, or stand some creeping inflation. If you can't tolerate unemployment, and if you insist upon reasonable price stability, there is nothing to do but bring government into the act, invoking formal or informal price-wage controls.

Two decades have passed and one must admit that the prophet's pessimism was amply justified. Indeed, he may not have been pessimistic enough. Perhaps even with government intervention, we cannot long enjoy both high employment and reasonable price stability. That is the basic issue we face here tonight.

Since I have quoted one prophet and am here performing the role of the devil's advocate, let me now quote another prophet, John Kenneth Galbraith. Not content with the fame and affluence from his earlier works, Galbraith has brought forth a new classic, *The New Industrial State*. From it we can learn his views on the subject of guideposts.

> At any reasonably high level of demand, prices and wages in the industrial system are inherently unstable. . . . The . . . remedy for the wage-price spiral is to regulate prices and wages by public authority. . . . In World War II and the Korean War . . . the wage-price spiral was successfully contained by controls. . . . [and] there was nothing unique about the war-time situation. Economic institutions and behavior are not drastically altered either by declared or undeclared war. . . .
>
> This initiative [of guideposts] was, perhaps, the most important innovation in economic policy of the administration of President John F. Kennedy. . . . Thereafter for several years the wage guideposts, as they came to be called, and the counterpart price behavior were a reasonably accepted feature of government policy. Wage negotiations were closely consistent with the guidelines. Prices of manufactured goods were stable.

Let me quote another modern prophet, Milton Friedman, whose palette holds different paint:

> Inflation is always and everywhere a monetary

phenomenon. . . . It follows that the only effective
way to stop inflation is to restrain the rate of growth
of the quantity of money. . . . Compliance with the
guideposts is harmful because it encourages delay in
taking effective measures to stem inflation, distorts
production and distribution, and encourages restric-
tions on personal freedom . . . guidelines threaten
the censensus of shared values which is the moral
basis of a free society.[2]

I suppose it will be argued by many that Professors
Galbraith and Friedman are not middle-of-the-road
men. Let me, therefore, demonstrate the capacity of our
subject for arousing strong opinion by quoting Arthur
F. Burns:

The fundamental point of the preceding analysis
is that general observance of the guideposts would
throttle the forces of competition no less effectively
than those of monopoly. . . . Since free competitive
markets would virtually cease to exist in an economy that observed the guidelines, this transforma-
tion of the economy merits serious reflection.[3]

Let us begin by clearing up one inexcusable misunder-
standing of the wage guideposts. After President Kennedy issued his 1962 recommendation that wage rates be
increased only by the 3.2 percent increase in labor productivity, financial columnists and corporate executives
repeatedly stated in an arithmetical falsity:

If labor productivity grows by 3.2 percent and
wages rise by 3.2 percent, then there is zero percent
left over of the fruits of technological progress to
go to profit. And yet much, probably most, of the
improvement in labor productivity is in fact attrib-

utable to better capital tools, better management methods, and improved scientific know-how.

Indeed it would be unfair and unworkable if all the fruits of progress were to go to labor alone. The guide-lines could be rejected out of hand were this their purpose and effect. But critics who use this argument have failed in their elementary arithmetic. The truth is that a 3 percent increase in labor productivity matched by a 3 percent increase in wages entails exactly a 3 percent in-crease in profits. To clinch this, suppose we begin with 700 of wages and 300 of profit, or 1,000 in all. Let pro-ductivity grow by 3 percent, so that we now have 1,030 to divide. A 3 percent increase in wages does not use up the whole of the extra 30, but rather .03 × 700 = 21, with 9 left over the profit. But what is this 9? It is exactly .03 × profit's original 30. Those financial col-umnists who wept crocodile tears for euthanaesia of the profit class engendered by guidelines could have been saved from error if the presidential directive had been enunciated as a 3.2 percent increase in profits *and* wages.

In economic argumentation, when you gain one friend you lose another. Precisely because the guidelines allow for an equal percentage increase in all factor-of-produc-tion shares, they have been criticized as "freezing the *status quo* distribution of productive incomes." I must confess that this was my initial reaction against them.

What is so sacred about the existing distribution of income that it should be frozen forever? For one thing, why should organized labor agree in perpetuity to desist

from trying to raise the share of the social pie going to
workers? And, if you believe that it is the purely competitive forces of the marketplace which determine the
distribution of income shares, what a coincidence it
would be for changes in technology and tastes to be
such as lead exactly to perpetuation of any base-period
sharing of the national income?

My qualms in this matter, and those of any critic,
seem to be best answered by quoting the analysis of
Professor Robert Solow, one of the formulators of the
Kennedy guideposts.

> It seems to me that this argument has no practi-
> cal weight at all. It is rendered trivial by two facts.
> The first is that the division of the national income
> between labor and property incomes is among the
> slower-changing characteristics of our economy, or
> of any Western economy. The second is that neither
> the guideposts nor any other such quantitative pre-
> scription can be satisfied exactly. Suppose that wage
> rates do follow the guideposts exactly. Then if the
> price level, instead of remaining constant, goes up
> by, say, 1 percent in a year, the share of wages in
> national income will fall by 1 percent—that is, by
> about ¾ of 1 percentage point. If, on the other
> hand, the price level should fall by 1 percent, the
> share of wages in national income would rise by ¾
> of 1 percentage point. That may not seem like
> much, but actually it is quite a lot, more than
> enough to provide all the flexibility that our eco-
> nomic system is likely to need.
>
> In the twenty years since the end of the war, the
> proportion of "compensation of employees" to na-
> tional income has moved about within a narrow

range, say from 65 percent to 71 percent. There is no reason to suppose that market forces will always want to keep the figure within those bounds, but there is every reason to believe that market forces will never, or hardly ever, want to move the proportional distribution of income very rapidly. As the numerical example shows, if wages adhered to the guidelines, the distribution of income could get from one end of its postwar range to the other in about eight years, with an annual rate of inflation or deflation never exceeding 1 percent.[4]

Since this is a seminar, I trust I shall be forgiven for writing down a few simple equations or arithmetical identities. The value of total product is equal to dollar-price times quantity sold; and this can be broken up into wage-cost alone plus the remainder, which is the share of profit.[5]

$$P \times Q = W \times L + \text{Profit}$$

Now let us write the ratio depicting the relative share of profits to wages as r. Then arithmetic multiplication and division and a little rearrangement of terms will convert our equation into the guidepost form.

$$W = P \left(1 + r\right) \left(\frac{Q}{L}\right)$$

This says that, if the price level is to be stable and relative factor shares are not to be disturbed, wage rates can rise only in the same proportion as physical-labor productivity rises. I warn that this is a mere tautology of arithmetic. In *any* inflation, even that of purest demand pull, wage rates and money profits rise at a faster pace than physical productivity.

The above formulation permits me to concede at once certain valid objections to any one frozen guidepost target number such as 3.2 percent. If business is to be subject to higher tax rates—as for example in the 1965 step-up in social security payroll tax rates—then permitting labor a wage-rate increase fully equal to the productivity increase would be in effect to say: "Labor is to bear none of the burden of the extra social security benefits voted by Congress." I agree that that would be unfair, but add the reminder that this is a two-way street. When Congress reduces business taxes—as in the investment tax credit—labor gets none of the benefits under frozen guidepost numbers.

The same problem arises from changes in prices of nonindustrial materials. When 1965 copper and oil prices rise, any firm experiencing only a 3.2 increase in the productivity of its *own* laborers can afford to raise its workers' wages by 3.2 percent only by suffering a deterioration of relative profit share.

Because the guideposts were promulgated in a period that proved to be an exceptionally long economic expansion, with productivity and volume continuing to grow for an exceptionally long time, one could not prior to 1967 weep for the plight of the profit receiver. Profits in the 1960s have done very well. But I must point out that in the course of the business cycle there is a characteristic fluctuation of the wage-profit share: the profit share drops during recessions and pauses; it rises sharply in recoveries. Thus, we must question whether the remarks quoted from Solow fully succeed in banishing concern that guidepost formulas tend to resist natural economic forces by trying to freeze relative factor shares. This is one way of looking at the problem which vexed President Johnson's advisers. To give, at the end of a cycle, wage increases equal to average productivity growth over the cycle, is to produce inflation at the end of the cycle. On the other hand, to hold down wage increases at the end of the cycle to the low productivity advances of that period is to fly in the face of tight labor markets and invite noncompliance with the guideposts.

Let me turn from the arithmetic of the problem to what it is that wage-price guideposts are an attempt to do.

A BETTER PHILLIPS CURVE

I cannot stress too strongly that wage-price guideposts are not substitutes for proper macroeconomic fiscal and monetary policies. Economists have always known that excessively easy monetary policy and/or enlarged expenditures coupled with small tax receipts can produce demand-pull inflation. The only cure for that situation is tighter money and/or more restrictive fiscal policy.

If prices and wages were perfectly flexible, like those in ideal auction markets, there would be no need for guideposts. The authorities would engineer fiscal and monetary expansion just up to the point of full employment. Prior to that point, the general price level would not rise and average wages would grow automatically with productivity. Relative prices and wages would have to show fluctuations in order to clear particular markets. In this ideal world, which differs dramatically from every mixed economy that now exists, the problem would be merely one of macroeconomic dosage, and there would be no dilemmas of policy.

Our mixed economy—like that of Germany, Japan, England, France, Sweden, and Belgium—reveals a tendency for prices to creep upward even when there is substantial unemployment. To keep wholesale prices stable and the implicit-GNP-deflator index growing at a moderate 1.5 percent might well require that U. S. unemployment be, in the short run, 5 percent or more.

Experience suggests that in the short run there is a trade-off between the intensity of unemployment of men and capital and the intensity of price increase. This can be plotted as a statistical scatter diagram and graphed in the form of what is called a Phillips curve—named after Professor A. W. Phillips of the London School of Economics, who measured this relationship for the United Kingdom over the past century. One must not exaggerate the exactitude of the Phillips curve but nevertheless it is one of the most important concepts of our times. Any criticism of the guideposts which does not explicitly take into account the Phillips curve concept

I have to treat as having missed the fundamental point of all economic policy discussions.

Let me illustrate with a case in point. I have quoted Friedman's view that the quantity theory of money is all-important in explaining fluctuations of aggregate spending. Suppose we grant a premise that I regard as untenable, namely that the velocity of circulation of money can be treated as a constant. Then the GNP can be rewritten as MV and by hypothesis it will move in strict proportion to the supply of M. One can still imagine two mixed economies that would differ drastically in their behavior with respect to creeping inflation. To put the matter succinctly, Economy A might have a very bad Phillips curve and Economy B might have a very good one. In Economy B the monopoly power of price-administrating corporations and of union bargainers is hardly to be observed at all. Employment can be very full indeed before the price level creeps. The problem of macroeconomic policy is the transparent one of dosage.

But how can we make mixed Economy A like that of B?

Now, maybe guideposts won't do it, which is a question that has to be examined on its merits. But don't make the mistake of thinking that macroeconomic policy can do it.

Macroeconomic policy can determine *where* you are on the Phillips curve. But if you have a bad short- or long-run curve, macroeconomic policy cannot give you a good Phillips curve.

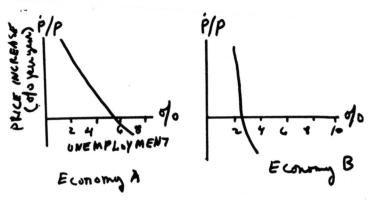

Figure 1. On the left is shown a typical Phillips curve for a mixed economy like that of the United States. By contrast, on the right is shown Economy B with a more ideal Phillips curve. The problem posed for guidelines and for "income policies" generally is not where one should be on the Phillips curve; that is the problem of proper macroeconomic fiscal and monetary policy. Rather the guideposts attempt to achieve a better Phillips curve—to shift the curve leftward so that it will be more like that of Economy B. This is also the problem for antitrust enforcement, for labor legislation, for avoidance of too-high minimum wage laws, for manpower retraining, and mobility programs.

Now, how can you get a good Phillips curve? And by a good Phillips curve I mean how can you get an economy which takes every expansion of purchasing power short of full employment and converts it into real, physical product of things that people want, an economy which lowers structural unemployment before prices creep. That's the problem for guideposts.

And that is why I think it is of the utmost superficiality for some people to say guideposts worked well from 1962 to 1964 but that they worked very badly in 1965, 1966, and 1967.

For prices to behave well in 1962-64 is a very easy victory, and it is not a victory that necessarily belongs to guideposts. And for guideposts to be judged to work badly in 1965 and 1966, you can't ask whether prices crept upward. You have to ask how prices and wages would have behaved in the absence of incomes policy or guideposts.

One may fairly ask what it is that critics of guideposts themselves advocate to meet this genuine problem of cost inflation.

We can all agree that the government should be careful in the way it spends its money so as not to drive up prices. And, of course, it would be nice to have better antitrust laws. I think we're all in favor of that. And if you know some way of making union behavior more like that of Economy B, then that will be very welcome. But the proposals that have been put forth, in terms of their actual feasibility, have not yet amounted to much.

The guideposts and related "incomes policies" are attempts all over the world to give us the same degree of fullness of employment with less price creep than would otherwise have been the case.

STATISTICAL ANALYSIS OF GUIDEPOSTS

Now, how would you judge whether guideposts have been influential? If this were a physical science, you might hope to make a controlled experiment, run the thing twice, with guideposts and without guideposts, and then see what the difference is. Of course, we can't do that.

One attempt by statistical multiple correlation, much quoted, was done on the subject at the Massachusetts Institute of Technology by George Perry of the University of Minnesota.

Perry first did what many people have done, such as Phillips in England. He tried to find a formula to estimate wage increases in the United States statistically. Then he related wage increases statistically to the degree of unemployment and to the amount of profits—because if the profits are very high, then concessions are given to wages—and to rates of change of these variables. This is a very familiar exercise.

I can't remember the exact date of his investigation, but I think he first used data that went up to about 1962 or 1963.

Then, on the basis of these previously established patterns, he tackled the post-1962 period in which the guideposts were operating. A number of other people have done the same thing and with much the same results.

All of these studies show that prices and wages did not rise as much in 1964, 1965, and 1966 as had been predicted for them on the basis of previous experience. For the same levels of unemployment, profitability, rates of change, and so forth, in post-1962 we did seem to have a better Phillips curve.

What was different? Well, some people say what was different were the Kennedy-Johnson guideposts. Now, that is not a conclusive argument. We can certainly think of some other things that were different. One is that in the late 1950s we ran a very sluggish economy. This has been called an investment in sadism by the old William McChesney Martin—not the new William Mc-Chesney Martin.

Although I call it an investment in sadism, it wasn't done just for kicks, and it may have had a return. Some can argue that one of its returns was the fact that we had a better Phillips curve in the 1960s under Kennedy and Johnson because of the unemployment that was tolerated in the 1950s by Eisenhower, i.e., differences in *past* his-tory, which are not in Perry's regressions, might possibly explain it.

I think if that were the case, I would expect as the passage of time goes on that this would be a fading type of effect; and it isn't clear to me that with the passage of time this has been the case.

I don't know how you feel about the present mid-1967 wage settlements and how they are going; but 12 months ago, if you had described today's tight labor market to me and asked me to predict how the wage settlements would be going, I would have thought, frankly, they would be higher than they have been.

I do want to mention one other factor, though, which is also different and which doesn't show in Perry's re-gression. That is the balance-of-payments constraint and the possible constraint on our prices and wages that come from the import picture.

As an example, I don't believe that the difference in behavior of the steel industry in the 1960s and the 1950s can be understood without reference to the import picture. I think socially the steel industry has been behaving immeasurably better in the 1960s than in the 1950s. And for the purpose of this argument I am not saying that this is because of a confrontation between President Kennedy and Roger Blough. Moreover I'm talking about better performance on the part of the union and the industry generally. I suspect that part of the reason is that the workers are beginning to realize that when they raise money wages and when that increases steel prices, they lose volume of business and employment.

And so a better Phillips curve in the 1960s—if indeed we have it—may be due to the openness of the economy and to the international competition.

Yet when all is said and done, I think that there is some influence discernible from the guidepost philosophy. Last year at a Chamber of Commerce debate, I described the guideposts as really an attempt to affect the philosophy of men in the marketplace.

Now, if you think that the marketplace is subject only to Walrasian equations of perfect competition, then the will of men, except as it affects our tastes between cheese and apples and clothing, will cancel out of everything and nobody's influence can make a difference. Then there is certainly no room for the guideposts.

By contrast, I think that there are many sectors in our modern mixed economy where the short-run behavior of people can be substantially affected through moral suasion and public attitudes.

But, if it were just that, these effects would probably be very short run. Remember, in these industrial sectors, as elsewhere, the whole is the sum of its parts. And if in the short run all of the oligopolies can be persuaded to take things easy on the upside with respect to price, that makes it much easier for every one of them to go along with this philosophy.

Sometimes what I am talking about is called the apologetics of the modern corporation. An old friend of mine from Japan once told me in the postwar period that if Japanese capitalism were like the new American capitalism, then he would not be a Socialist. He said "You are a rich country, which can afford a more gentle kind of capitalism."

The hard-boiled believers in markets say that this is rot, capitalism is just as bad as it ever was—by which they mean just as good as it ever was; they say, "The worst thing in the world would be for capitalists to stop acting like capitalists, to stop maximizing profits and start doing what it isn't their business to do. Don't believe them when they say they are doing it: in the first place they are lying; in the second place, they don't know what they are saying; and in the third place, if they really act that way, they won't be here tomorrow, because competition will take care of them."

Again by contrast, I think that there is a lot of cushion in the 500 largest corporations, which permits them to follow independent policy that takes some account of the public welfare.

I don't think you can expect the president of American Tobacco to get religion on lung cancer. I think that if he gets a violent view about cigarettes and lung cancer, he must go; he cannot stay as president of American Tobacco. He can't take the company with him, he has to go. But I don't think that is the situation in which the typical large corporation is. Here I am not talking about a single corporation trying to buck the system, because if one corporation behaved this way and no other corporation did, I agree that ruthless competition might soon eliminate it. But if all the 500 corporations in some degree have a social philosophy and purpose, I think that they enable each one to perform in this way.

One of my former students who works for one of the largest corporations in the world tried to get his board of directors there to admit that they maximize their profits. He said, "Profits aren't a dirty word. All I want you to do is admit that you maximize your long-run profits. And that it's good public relations in the long run to maximize your profits." Yet, he tells me, he cannot get them to admit that, adding, "And why not? These people have been in this large corporation all their executive lives; they have a lot of headaches, but by no means is their biggest headache the annual meeting. And when they say that they regard themselves as *pluralisti-*

cally responding to government, to their consumers, to their workers, and to their stockholders, after years of trying to get them to say the opposite I felt forced to believe them."

Now, the background of my argument that guideposts have some effect is that all the large corporations together and the labor unions do have some discretionary power in marking up their prices. While their sectors could charge what the market will bear, every time the demand seems to be inelastic, raising the prices, I don't recognize that as realistic for the large-corporation sector. I think you can get a price spiral in which all the large corporations simultaneously goad each other into raising prices. I extend this same argument, by the way, to the wage part of the picture.

Now, mind you, guideposts have been shown not to be a substitute for macroeconomic policy. You cannot print trillions of marks or dollars per day and think that public spirit is going to hold prices stable. But what you can do is have a system which at 5 percent unemployment generates creeping inflation of 3 percent per year, or one which at 5 percent unemployment generates a lower rate of price increase, being able to go to 4 percent of unemployment and still generate reasonable stability in the price index.

I regard the Galbraith quotation as absurd—that during the big war we held prices down and it worked well; that during the Korean War we held prices down and it worked well; that there is no real difference between war and peace, so let's just hold prices and wages down. The more you are trying to push the Phillips curve down, while also operating in the inflationary part of it, the less the situation can be maintained, particularly in the longer run. But within limits I think that the experience of the 1960s suggests to us that there has been an important role to be played by these informal controls.

WHAT LONG-RUN PHILLIPS CURVE?

Now, the time for my formal discussion is almost up, but I do raise a more complicated problem: How does the Phillips curve change over time?

I mentioned the hypothesis that unemployment in the late 1950s has made possible the good price behavior of the early 1960s. This can be expressed in different ways, and has been expressed in different ways. Professor Friedman in the cited volume expresses the matter this way: There is no tradeoff between unemployment and the rate of change of prices. (By that he means there is no such tradeoff, except in the short run.) Instead, he says, there is a tradeoff between today's unemployment and tomorrow's unemployment. And if you generate some unemployment today, you may be able to reduce unemployment tomorrow with the same price stability.

Now, I think that's true in part. I think that this effect is plausible from economic reasoning. I think there is some experience in the statistics which suggests that this is in fact the case.

But I do not think the sharper form of the doctrine is

true, namely that there is a one-to-one tradeoff between today's and tomorrow's unemployment. This would suggest enunciation of a new doctrine. We have the law of conservation of energy; we have the law of conservation of matter. We are now to have a new law of conservation, the alleged law of conservation of unemployment, which says: Any mixed economy has the same amount of unemployment to be enjoyed—if that is the right verb—over the long run regardless of price behavior, that it is the same whether in the long run you are averaging a 3 percent increase in the price level or stability in the price level, or a decrease in the price level.

If this notion of a vertical long-run Phillips curve were true, and if we like price stability and can afford the long-run view, then I suppose we might as well have stable prices and get this fundamental amount of unemployment at a stable price level.

You see what all this implies in terms of a Phillips curve diagram on this blackboard. We now have a vertical line at the structural amount of unemployment which is characteristic of the mixed economy in question. And independently of the price level you are always going to return to that same vertical line which represents the same fundamental amount of unemployment.

Of course, that line could conceivably be shifted. For example, trustbusting, getting rid of a minimum wage, promoting flexibility, making various structural changes, and educating the labor force might move the line to the left, but it is a vertical line regardless of price behavior.

I have been studying the time series trying to piece together from cases of experiences of different countries what I can. I also have been thinking of what is plausible. In the end I can't really see that it is plausible that unemployment should be a fundamental long-run constant, that there should be a one-to-one tradeoff.

I think it is true that you may gain in high employment in one short period and have to pay in some amount for it later. But I don't think that you need always pay an equal amount, and that the Phillips curve will reconstitute itself always at a perverse level, and at the same perverse level.

I hope that we'll get more scientific studies trying to elucidate this. The trouble is, of course, that experience is very slow to come by when we are trying to measure long-run relationships of this sort. And we rather hope that economies won't go through the fluctuations which will give us the experience that will add to our scientific knowledge, because the guinea pigs that the experiments will involve would be ourselves and our neighbors.

REBUTTALS

ARTHUR F. BURNS

The main point of Professor Samuelson's paper, as I read it, is that our government's wage and price guidelines—I prefer this term to guideposts—tend to restrain wage and price increases. Take two similar economies, Economy A which pursues a guidelines policy and Economy B which does not. At any given level of unemployment, wages and prices will tend to rise less in A than in B; so that A has more elbowroom for expansionist monetary and fiscal policies than B. It follows, therefore, that A will find it easier than B to approximate the twin objective of full employment and stability of the price level. This is the heart of Professor Samuelson's argument, and I believe he has made as good a case along these lines as can be made.

He has left me in doubt, however, on some essential points. I am not sure whether his cautious appraisal applies principally to the guidelines proclaimed by the Council of Economic Advisers in January, 1962, or to the rather different guidelines of January, 1964, or to the still different guidelines of January, 1967, or to all these versions. Nor can I tell whether his qualified approval of the guidelines applies to the enforcement

procedures used by the government as well as to the
principle or principles of the guidelines. Nor can I tell
whether he recognizes that, granting their promise, the
guidelines may also have perverse side effects—for example, by inducing some weak trade unions to hold out
for higher wages than they otherwise would, or by
inducing some business firms not to lower prices today
because of fear of criticism or reprisal if they restore
prices tomorrow, or by inducing this or that government
to pursue expansionist policies beyond what he calls the
"proper" point.

In view of these doubts, I will not dwell on the details
of Professor Samuelson's admirable paper. Nor do I in-
tend to dwell on my own position with regard to the
guidelines. My paper in the *Harvard Business Review,*
from which Professor Samuelson quoted, was devoted to
the guidelines policy set forth in 1964. That policy
called, in effect, for setting wages and prices by mathematical formula. That policy implied, or at least I so in-
terpreted it, either the sort of capricious enforcement
that we have had or more comprehensive procedures that
could permanently damage the efficiency of our economy. That policy also carried the danger, which I felt it
was important to emphasize, that expansionist measures
would be pushed in practice well beyond the proper
point. Neither the course of recent history nor Professor
Samuelson's defense has led me to change those views. On
the other hand, I have no quarrel with the sort of guidelines that were set forth in 1962, if they would only stay

that way and if we also were realistic enough not to expect very much from them. Thus, if Professor Samuelson stopped being the devil's advocate, he and I might not be very far apart.

In any event, if our own nation's or foreign experience is any guide, this or that set of guidelines is at best likely to make merely an occasional or marginal contribution to the problem of enabling our economy to realize over any considerable period both full employment and a stable price level. This problem has baffled economists and government officials for many years both in our country and elsewhere. The chances are that we will continue to struggle with it, and that we will have to try out many ideas, both new and old. Toward the end of the paper I presented here two weeks ago, I referred tersely to some of the things that we may need to do or consider, and I want to take advantage of the time at my disposal to elaborate a little on some of those thoughts.

One major need, as I see it, is to strengthen the forces and institutions of our society that favor high employment and reasonable price stability. Governmental fussing with minor changes in the performance of the economy may easily be ill-timed, prove ineffective or perverse, and therefore ultimately weaken the effectiveness of governmental policy in handling major problems. We have become too preoccupied with short-run variations of macroeconomic policy, and we do not give enough thought to creating and maintaining an environment that will lessen the burden of discretionary policy-making.

To begin with, the public interest would be well served if the government dismantled some of the impediments to competition which it has itself erected or fostered; that is, if it proceeded to reduce tariffs, eliminate import quotas, reduce farm price supports, discourage restrictive work practices, reform the minimum wage, and enforce the antitrust laws more strictly. Forthright and courageous attention to these matters would in my judgment do more to curb advances in the wage and price level than the guidelines on which we have recently been relying. Last year, for example, the government kept lecturing labor leaders on the importance of restraining wage increases, and yet it proceeded to raise the minimum wage and to bring many additional workers under this legal umbrella. Such a policy is not only inconsistent with the professed objective of price stability; it is blind or cynical as well. To be sure, a higher and more inclusive minimum wage will benefit those who keep or get jobs. But it will also exert upward pressure on the price level and it will restrict the employment opportunities of inexperienced and unskilled workers—who, I need hardly say, suffer most from unemployment. Indeed, our practical choice may soon be between higher unemployment of unskilled workers and a price level that is sufficiently high to validate in the marketplace the newly prescribed worth of marginal workers.

Besides attending better than we have to the need for

open and competitive markets, I believe that it would be desirable to strengthen the unemployment insurance system—which over the years has fully proved its usefulness as an automatic stabilizer. In 1958 and again in 1961, the Congress tardily enacted a temporary extension of unemployment insurance benefits. When the next recession strikes, as in time it probably will, our country should be equipped with an unemployment insurance system that at last covers practically all wage earners, that automatically provides for extended benefits during periods of abnormally large unemployment, and that guards against present abuses. It may also be helpful to devise some new automatic stabilizers. One possibility that deserves consideration is a stabilization fund to which individual workers would be required to contribute, and on which they could draw—to the extent that their personal accumulation plus earned interest permits—in the event of unemployment, retirement, or perhaps serious illness as well. Under such a scheme of compulsory saving, the credit balance of a worker would pass to his estate or to a designated beneficiary upon death.

But whether or not we proceed to strengthen the automatic stabilizers, we may well need some protection against their limitations. The stabilizers tend to cushion an economic decline automatically, and this is a good thing; but they also tend to check economic expansion automatically—and this is often undesirable. The latter tendency can be especially serious on account of our income tax, which is so highly productive of governmental revenue when the private economy is expanding that it may choke off the process of expansion prematurely. Fortunately, the latter tendency can be offset by a systematic policy of tax reduction. Once the war in Vietnam is over, reductions of income taxes will probably be needed, and it is not too early to consider what to do. I can think of no policy that is more likely to foster a steady advance of prosperity than the one spelled out in the preamble of the Revenue Act of 1964. In order to assure that such a policy will this time endure, legislative plans should provide for modest yearly tax reductions over a five- or ten-year period. The legislation should permit, however, some flexibility, and one way of achieving it would be to stipulate that the reduction specified for a given fiscal year will not go into effect if the President finds it undesirable and the Congress ratifies his decision.

I have commented thus far on a few of the ways in which the government can create conditions that will favor high employment and general price stability. There are other desirable changes, particularly in the financial area, such as the early reduction or removal of the gold cover against Federal Reserve notes; but time is insufficient to discuss them. Let me turn, therefore, to a second major problem area—namely, the need to improve the machinery and tools of economic policy-making.

In my lecture I noted how faulty statistics on prices

and the gross national product complicated the task of policymakers in 1965. Many other branches of our statistical system need improvement; and it may be especially pertinent, in view of the importance that the guidelines have assumed in the present discussion, to say a few words about wage statistics. The wage data that are followed most intensively by economists are the monthly figures on hourly earnings in manufacturing. These figures gave an accurate picture of wage levels and trends a generation ago, but they no longer do so. In the first place, they represent hours paid for rather than hours worked, and hence do not allow for the increasing number of hours that are paid for but not worked. Second, they exclude the cost of fringe benefits—a factor of large and increasing importance to employers and employees alike. Third, they exclude the sizable and increasing fraction of employees who are classified by official statisticians as "nonproduction" workers. It is also worth noting that employees in the goods-producing industries are now outnumbered by those in the service industries, and that the statistical coverage of wage rates and earnings in the service industries is meager. I do not think that our present wage statistics are capable of carrying the burden that the guidelines have imposed on them.

A still more serious deficiency of our economic intelligence system is the virtual lack of data on job vacancies. The Employment Act declares that the federal government has the responsibility of promoting "conditions under which there will be afforded useful employment opportunities . . . for those able, willing, and seeking to work." To discharge this responsibility, statistics are needed to determine to what degree, if any, the aggregate demand for labor falls short of the number of "those able, willing, and seeking to work." Clearly, the aggregate demand for labor includes the unfilled jobs as well as those that are being manned, just as the aggregate supply of labor includes the unemployed workers as well as those who have jobs. Hence, to determine the relation between aggregate demand and supply, data on job vacancies are every bit as essential as data on unemployment. If, at any particular time, unemployment exceeds job vacancies at prevailing wages, then the demand for labor is obviously insufficient to provide a job for everyone who is "able, willing, and seeking to work." At such a time, an expansionist economic policy is suited to the nation's domestic needs. On the other hand, when the number of vacant jobs is equal to or larger than the number of unemployed, there is no deficiency of aggregate monetary demand. A government that is seriously concerned about inflation will not seek to expand demand at such a time. Hence, if we equip ourselves in the future with the information needed to ascertain the true state of demand, and if we also devote far more effort than we have to securing better matching of the men and women who seek work with the jobs that need to be filled, we should be able to pursue the objective of full employment with less danger of causing serious inflation.

Once existing statistical information is improved and
the more obvious needs—such as systematic data on job
vacancies and short-run projections of the federal budget
—are provided for, it should be possible to improve the
economic forecasts on which discretionary policymaking
is so heavily based. Much research on forecasting techniques is going forward, but much more is needed. Forecasters have not yet learned how to take account of the
changing state of confidence, either in their equations
or in their practical judgments. Nor do they as yet know
enough about the timing or the magnitude of the re-
sponse of the economic system to shifts in monetary or
fiscal policy. Nor do they know enough to allow for
the momentum of economic forces in the private economy when they forecast the nation's output. Nor do
they always allow, as they might, for the cyclical behavior of productivity when they forecast such a subtle
magnitude as potential output. According to a study
by the National Bureau of Economic Research, profes-
sional forecasters erred, on the average, by $10 billion in
estimating the year-to-year change in the gross national product between 1952 and 1963. In view of this
finding, and I might note that the record of the best—
or luckiest—forecasters was not dramatically better, it
is highly important to keep in mind the present limitations of the art of economic forecasting, even as we try
to improve it.

I was surprised to learn this January that our governmental authorities believed that, while the economy

would remain sluggish in the first half of the year, so rapid a recovery was likely in the second half that a tax increase would be needed as of July 1, in order to restrain the expansion. Although intuitive forecasts sometimes turn out to be right, it is dangerous to base tax policy on such a contingency. It is possible, of course, that the forecast of our policymakers and their tax proposal were influenced by the prospect of a huge budgetary deficit. If so, I must confess to a momentary nostalgia for the "good old days" when a tax proposal of the sort made in January would have been defended in a straightforward manner on budgetary grounds.

Clearly, there is much work ahead for economists in improving the tools on which governmental policymakers rely in their efforts to promote prosperity without inflation. There is also work ahead for political scientists. In a far-flung government of divided powers, such as ours, it is not easy to achieve effective coordination of economic policies. Yet, it should be possible to do better than we did in 1956 or again in 1966, when failures of coordination became especially glaring. I have long felt that an Economic Cabinet could become a useful instrument of coordination, but I am by no means sure that this alone would prove a significant reform. On the other hand, I have grave doubts about the desirability of adding to the economic powers of the executive. Centralization of economic authority in the office of the President has its intellectual appeal, but let us not overlook the protection against the risk of concentrated error that the economy now derives from the dispersal of power in our governmental scheme.

In addition to dealing with the problem of coordination, political scientists might be helpful in devising better ways of mobilizing the forces of economic understanding and of bringing them to bear on policymaking. The reports of the Council of Economic Advisers have contributed very materially to this purpose, and so too have the hearings and scholarly studies of the Joint Economic Committee. These instrumentalities, however, have their limitations. No matter how excellent this or that report by the Council may be, it is by its very nature a political document and it may therefore be taken too seriously by some and not seriously enough by others. The hearings and studies by the Joint Economic Committee have the singular advantage of drawing on a wide range of economic thinking, but they are not read as widely or as closely as the reports of the Council. Many citizens, both within and outside the government, have therefore come to feel the need for guidance in economic matters that is more objective than the Council's reports and less diffused than the Committee's reports. One way of meeting this need would be to establish on a bipartisan basis a commission of economic experts whose major function would be to review, in the spirit of science, the economic reports of the President and the Council. Such a commission might be recreated each year on an *ad hoc* basis, or it might be given continuity. In either case, it would have to be independent of both the executive and the Congress. I need hardly add that there may be other and more effective ways of mobilizing knowledge in the interest of informed discussion of the true state and prospects of the nation's economy.

In summary, I see a need for creating conditions that will of themselves tend to favor high employment and reasonable price stability, so that the burden of discretionary policy may become lighter. At the same time, I fully recognize that whatever automatic or semi-automatic devices are eventually developed, the area for discretionary actions will remain large. That is why my lecture was devoted to monetary and fiscal policy and that is why I have commented so extensively today on the need for better tools of policymaking. Some of the devices that I have considered should serve to improve the Phillips curve, as Professor Samuelson likes to put it, directly. Others—among which a proper monetary and fiscal policy is basic—will tend to do so indirectly by serving to stretch out a relatively high degree of prosperity.

In discussing tools and institutions, I have said very little about the policymakers themselves or how their role might be improved. Surely, the best of tools will not of themselves assure good monetary and fiscal policies any more than crude tools will necessarily lead to poor policies. I wish I had a formula for arriving at wise discretionary policies, for I could then unveil it on this occasion. I know of no such formula or rule or set of rules. All that I can do is to submit a half-dozen practical observations for your judgment. First, frequent revisions of basic tax policies can be needlessly disturbing to private decision makers and they should be avoided as far as possible. Indeed, if it ever becomes governmental policy to move income tax rates up and down at very brief intervals, this rule of behavior will become a normal part of expectations and the effectiveness of fiscal policy will be drastically reduced. Second, abrupt shifts of monetary policy can easily cause economic imbalances, and they too should be avoided as far as possible. Third, since reductions of governmental expenditure are extremely difficult to achieve in practice, the most careful thought should be given to any proposed enlargements of expenditure. Fourth, "fine tuning" of economic policy is a hazardous art in the present state of economic knowledge. Fifth, unless signs of inflation are recognized and respected at an early stage by the makers of monetary and fiscal policy, troublesome economic imbalances are soon likely to pile up. Finally, free markets are our nation's most valuable economic asset and we should therefore be wary of governmental edicts, perhaps all the more so when they come in the coquettishly modern dress of voluntary guidelines.

PAUL A. SAMUELSON

Last Tuesday when I spoke here I characterized myself as a middle-of-the-road man and I characterized Arthur Burns as a middle-of-the-road man, and I said that sometimes we are so much alike that I am not sure that I don't cross over to the other side of him.

At that time, I had not read his paper. I didn't have the privilege of hearing it the previous week. One of the more fortunate members of this audience said to me, "You may be both in the middle of the road but you have been talking about entirely different subjects; there is very little resemblance between the topics that you have chosen to deal with and those that Arthur Burns dealt with last week."

So I had the task of saying to myself, sort of a Walter Mitty task, "If I were Arthur Burns, what would I say on the subject that I didn't talk about?" And I turned out to be a pretty good prophet, as judged by my reading of his speech.

I felt a little bit like the old farmer who came to town and heard Aristotle speak. When he was asked what he thought about Aristotle, he said, "I thought he was pretty good and, as a matter of fact, I thought he was expounding some of my best ideas."

ONCE-AND-FOR-ALL IMPROVEMENTS

There is very much for me to agree with in Burns' speech of two weeks ago, which text I have now read, and with what he said here today.

For example, I listened to his Five-Point Program for improving, if you want to put it this way, the Phillips curve. Reducing tariffs and quotas, I am for that. For lowering farm price supports. Like 95 percent of the economists polled by the Chase Manhattan Bank, it turns out that we all are for that. A girl in Wisconsin once wrote to me and said, "Sir, what is it you have against the Merchant Marine? Your animus shows."

Just recently a University of Maryland student wrote to me and said, "Your ill-disguised contempt for the farmer comes through in everything that you write." Well, I don't think that I'm against the kind of farm price support program that we have had just because I don't like farmers. There is no difference between us on that point.

If somebody has a good method for improving work practices in American industry, I would like to hear about it and I would like to endorse it.

I know that just introducing into a major collective bargaining dispute a requirement that there be better work practices in some years is about the best way devised to get a *bad* Phillips curve in that year. It can take a union rank and file who isn't very militant on money-wage increases and turn it into a lynching mob, as in the case of the 1959 steel strike when "work rules" became an issue.

I am also in favor of more successful enforcement of the antitrust acts and, in particular, the antitrust acts that increase competition and not those which reduce competition.

When it comes to the minimum wage, I always welcome that as a rare opportunity to appear as a reactionary in any discussion. I fear the consequences of too high a minimum wage. We had a candidate for governor in Massachusetts who outdid almost anyone because he came out for a $2 minimum wage and, when he was told that that was a lot to ask for Massachusetts, he said, I'm for a $2 minimum wage for the workers all over the world.

I wrote to him—he happened to be a learned professor—and said, "There isn't anything that the devil could devise that would do more harm to this globe than to enforce a $2 minimum wage all around the world, although that indeed would be to the benefit of Massachusetts, if it were done."

I am for strengthening the unemployment insurance system and a number of other matters of that sort.

I don't think, excellent as those ideas are, that all of them will be implemented and I do not believe that by themselves they will solve the dilemma in a mixed economy of an incomes policy. Moreover, to take just the first of these, the reductions of tariffs and quotas, that, of course, is a once-and-for-all thing. If we, in fact, could quench the fires of one budding inflation by reducing tariffs and quotas down to zero, we would have shot our bolt. It is not something that you can do again and again. However, for the long pull of getting tariffs and quotas down, I can't imagine a better way of doing it than on the occasions when we have over-full employment and an overly tight labor market. That is the time to make some progress in this matter.

Still, what is one of the most important reasons why we want to keep creeping inflation from taking place at all, or from creeping as fast as it creeps in years like 1965? I think that virtue is worth pursuing for its own sake. But, in addition, it is the balance of payments that makes us desire that our creeping inflation and our increase in wage costs not go in excess of those of other countries. And, since I have a suspicion that the dollar may be in some degree overvalued—as could be tested in the abstract by a floating exchange rate to see whether it would move up or whether it would move down—I am not sure that at this stage of history we really can afford a sizable reduction in tariffs and quotas.

And my own fear is that, as time develops, we will get a renascence of protectionist sentiment. We see it in the textile industry and we see it in the steel industry. Nevertheless, I am in favor of gradual reduction in barriers to trade.

THE NEW LOOK IN ECONOMICS

Let me move on, because this is to be a debate, even though a rational debate, and I shouldn't make it a love fest. I ought to try to find some difference of opinion in the excellent review of the 1950s and the 1960s that Arthur Burns put before you a couple of weeks ago.

I would like to start out and say that I agree that the late 1950s was a period of a rather sluggish American economy; and that one of the reasons for this was indeed the fear of the authorities over the creeping inflation which was then in evidence. Particularly, the 1957-58 experience was disquieting. At a time when labor markets weren't tight, you still had prices and wages creeping.

So I can understand that the Federal Reserve and the executive branch were tempted to move in the direction of austerity even though, as I would put it, they were led to cross the line into being overly sadistic.

Second, I also want to agree that the Kennedy-Johnson America of the 1960s did derive considerable benefit from this investment in sadism by the second Eisenhower Administration. I don't mean merely to joke, but President Kennedy's predecessor made him look good. I think that this was true because of Eisenhower's inactivism and errors of omission. But also he created conditions which were helpful to the long expansion which we have had in the 1960s and which perhaps we still are having.

Now let me comment on the change in thinking which Arthur Burns, I think correctly, discerns in the new economists. There was a distinct move to change the emphasis away from business-cycle thinking towards long-term-trend and growth thinking. This can be illustrated by the task force which I headed for President-elect Kennedy at the turn of the year between 1960 and 1961. It's not a secret, at least it's not a secret any more, that the majority of this task force was in favor of a tax cut at that time.

This was a notion which was shocking to the men around President Kennedy and it was shocking to President Kennedy himself. There was one perfectly good psychological reason for this shock.

John F. Kennedy had asked the country for sacrifices in his speech in Detroit on Labor Day and, for the first time, his campaign seemed to get off the ground. You should have seen the President-elect's face when told that the first sacrifice he should ask of the American people was to accept a tax-cut handout. It took a great deal of, shall I say education and rational debate to change that viewpoint. The confrontation with the leaders of the steel industry in the first part of 1962 may have also contributed to President Kennedy's conversion to the course of a massive tax cut. Perhaps that steel incident—none of us can be sure—had something to do with the intensification of the stock market decline in April and May of 1962.

I am not clairvoyant, but I think that suddenly the President realized that, if we went into a recession, he was the one who was going to be blamed, rightly or wrongly, for this; so, despite some of his reservations with respect to budget deficits and orthodox budget constraints—for which, at the end, Arthur Burns expressed some nostalgia, and for which I express no nostalgia—this 1962 incident may have pushed him over the line politically into deciding for a tax reduction. I think intellectually he had been converted earlier than that.

To go back to that task force, we were in no doubt that the recession of 1960-61 would come to an end within 1961. The consensus, and it was a strong consensus, was that this would probably take place by the middle of the year. But little did we realize how powerful was our new peerless leader, that he could take office on January 27th and by February 15th turn the whole business cycle situation around so that Geoffrey Moore would mark a National Bureau turning point so soon.

But, nevertheless, our predictions were in that ballpark and still we were in favor of a tax cut. We were in favor of expansionist programs even though the recession were to be over. Contrast our view with the advocacy, which some wise men made in 1957-58, of a tax cut.

The notion then was that we were in a recession in 1957-58 and that there should be a tax reduction. You will recall that the Congress went home at Easter time. It turned out the country was not hurting and not demanding a tax increase, and that tax increase never did come about prior to the April upturn.

Many people who had advocated a tax cut said it should have been done earlier but now it's too late; and they were right, if they meant by that, too late in terms of a National Bureau recovery. At least by hindsight, they were right. I emphasize "by hindsight" because many people now claim they knew that Geoffrey Moore was going to declare an upturn and a revival around April of 1958. However, an acquaintance of mine who was speculating heavily in the government bond market and who told me he had two years' income hanging on the results was canvassing all of his friends in Washington in high and low places, as late as May and June, 1958, and he says, "Don't believe them when they tell you that they were sure that the turn had come."

Nevertheless, it was in the air that something like bottom had been reached and so, if you had been in favor of a tax reduction only for cyclical purposes, the time was past for that. But from this longer-run viewpoint of growth, of reducing—if I may use the new-economics jargon—the "gap," then it was not too late in April of 1958 for a tax cut and it was not too late for one in 1961.

If I could remake history, having the wisdom of hindsight, I think we should have had massive tax reductions after the Korean War, not small ones. We might then have had an entirely different kind of 1950s, including leaving the legacy to the 1960s of the high employment environment with which we are now grappling tonight. We would earlier have confronted the problem of how you can have over a considerable period of time in a mixed economy like ours both low levels of unemployment and reasonable price stability.

HIGH-EMPLOYMENT GOAL VERSUS PRICE STABILITY

Now, as I read the chronicle of the 1960s as described by Dr. Burns, I think that on most of the facts and most of the interpretations I would be in very close agreement with him.

There are some differences in our policy prescriptions. I'd say that I have been more of a "high-pressure" man than Dr. Burns. I would be very surprised if we would ever both be at a meeting of the Federal Reserve and I would say they should be cutting down and Arthur Burns would be saying they should be pouring it on. That's not usually the configuration that takes place in such meetings.

This involves value judgments. It involves value judgments as to the importance, in the short run, of marginal-worker, youth, and Negro unemployment. It also involves practical questions that none of us are able to answer and which I only scratched the surface of last week, the long-term Phillips curve—what the relationship is between unemployment today and unemployment tomorrow, and whether you in the longer run minimize the level of unemployment by tolerating a little more unemployment in the present.

Now, there are differences of opinion and emphasis between me and Dr. Burns. It would be idle for me to say that in the present state of economic knowledge I have confidence that he is wrong and I am right; but I think we should record and note these particular differences.

ROLE OF CONFIDENCE

Within the framework of analysis there is a more minor point that I would like to comment on. Arthur Burns just happened to mention it very briefly today. That is the problem of confidence. What is the role of business confidence for the analyst, quite aside from approving or disapproving, but just in understanding the course of events?

Sometimes I am reminded a bit of the question that Napoleon put to Laplace, after Laplace had finished his great treatise on celestial mechanics. Napoleon said to Laplace, "What is the role of God in your system?" And the Marquis de Laplace said, "God? I have no use for that hypothesis, sire." Lagrange was heard to whisper under his breath, "Ah, but what a beautiful hypothesis."

I sometimes think about the role that the confidence factor plays in my regressions. I am not now referring to the regressions of the computer but I am speaking now of the regressions of the mind, the intuitive forecasting which I do. The other day a colleague of mine, Ed Kuh, said to me, "Paul, how long do you think it will take before a computer will replace you?" This is because I had just shown him some marvelous printouts that we get now from certain government agencies, which give you the GNP for the next four quarters as an IBM print-

out. "How long will it take before a computer will replace me?" I thought for a moment, and as the question
seemed to be asked in a mean way, I replied, "Not in a
million years."

I could be off by a factor of ten—but I still stick to
the intuitive regression equations of my mind and ask
myself quite seriously: "What is the role of confidence
in them?"

I am reminded again of a very brilliant mathematician
who was a Junior Fellow at Harvard at the same time
that I was, Stanislaw Ulam, one of the developers of the
hydrogen bomb and one of the world's greatest mathe-
maticians, then in the full flower of his mathematical
youth and vigor. Ulam told me that he had worked out
a formula for success in life, and that there were many
factors in the formula. Relevant factors included how
hard you worked, how good looking you were, who your
father-in-law was, what your natural ability was, and
so forth. He said though, that with respect to the factor
of natural ability, he had manipulated the formula and
manipulated it until finally he found that natural ability
entered in both the numerator and denominator so that
he could cancel it right out of the equation.

I jest with a purpose. I am not convinced that confidence merits much of an independent role for the
analyst.

For one thing there is a problem of defining confidence. At the most trivial level it is how businessmen feel
in after-business hours about the President. That index

of confidence goes up and down. I have friends in the financial community who have kept book, looseleaf notebooks, on the 72 unfriendly acts of President Kennedy between inauguration day and the steel confrontation. At one period you have a honeymoon period and the businessmen are friendly toward the President. You have an alleged consensus. And then that goes away. Now, I think this sort of radioactive background count of presidential popularity is one of the less important meanings of the word "confidence."

On the other hand, if you mean by confidence whether businessmen think there will be profitability of a dollar investment, then, that kind of confidence, I don't think is made by sweet talk and speeches, nor do I think it is easily unmade by even gross acts of indiscretion by the Chief Executive.

My old teacher and professor, Schumpeter, used to comment, on the whole in an admiring way, about the business annals. He would quote how the death of Queen Victoria's consort was explained by Bagehot as the cause of some crisis in Lombard Street, and he would laugh at that.

I think that confidence in the sense of profitability almost follows its own laws without respect to what goes on in Washington. I don't mean that you can't kill confidence by punitive tax laws or, if TVA builds a generator in your county, that this is going to leave the marginal efficiency of capital of private public utilities in that county undisturbed.

But I recall having pointed out to me the annual reports of Monsanto Chemical, a young and growing company in the 1930s, headed at that time by a very young, vigorous, strongly opinionated businessman, Mr. Queeny. Mr. Queeny was in favor of Franklin Roosevelt at the time of the 1932 election. We have forgotten what those times were like. There were a number of businessmen who turned New Dealers in a very radical way.

He said, in his annual report just before the inauguration, "Things are terrible, the country is in awful shape but there is hope on the horizon. We have a young, vigorous President, determined to do the right thing and we look forward to a new year with confidence."

Then, at the end of the next year, his annual report said: "Profits are in the black; they are immeasurably better than last year. However, we see on the horizon certain ominous signs of the octopus of Washington." So these quotations went. Each year Monsanto Chemical expanded tremendously, its share price went up in the stock market; it did the business of the GNP in a magnificent way. And yet the dyspepsia with the Washington administration grew as the private profits grew.

Now, I rather prefer to believe, and this is on the basis of plausible reasoning and experience, that there will be found a small role for confidence. After all your views with respect to profitability can be affected by political events. But, when I look at the residuals that I have to explain after I have used the plausible variables of economic analysis, I am not sure that I find residuals there which need to be correlated with the factor of confidence. Just to make this a debate, let me say that I am not sure that the delay in the revival of fixed plant and equipment expenditure in early 1961-62 is not adequately explained when you put in the variables of profitability, taking into account the overhang of capacity from the previous investment boom. I question whether the R^2 which you get without the factor of confidence—the coefficient of determination or fraction of explained variance—would be sizably in need of improvement and capable of improvement by the factor of confidence. Still, that's a small matter.

THE NEW ECONOMICS

I want to go back to what I think divides us new economists from—I can't really think of everyone else as old economists—from other economists. It is our activist attempts to stretch out the prosperity periods by explicit action.

Since everybody talks about "me and Kennedy," let me relate that one of the things that astonished me most in 1961 was how the lawyers in the Kennedy Administration really believed their own rhetoric—that the country was going to get moving by speaking about getting it moving; and it was a great surprise and required some education for them to realize that you had really to *do* things to achieve vigorous growth and prosperity.

Actually, many things were done from the very beginning in 1961. Expenditures were deliberately expanded.

There was a great deal of—I hesitate to call it hypocrisy —but of semantic double talk because there was a great deal of need for the country to adjust itself to rational fiscal thinking. Thus the desire for the investment tax credit by the Kennedy Administration was a genuine desire to stimulate investment by giving away revenue, even though, for window dressing purposes, it was sometimes thought necessary to couple it with revenue-raising verbiage. Eventually too we had the accelerated depreciation guidelines of mid-1963.

Every time the economy showed signs of flagging, other programs were introduced. It seems to me the dynamics of the private economy are not much different from what they were 20, 30, or 40 years ago. I think the businessmen were not dumb then. I think that they are smarter now and they do have better control over inventories; but this could give us, in some models, sharper and quicker inventory cycles than before.

The big change is this, and it could have been made in the last half of the 1950s, had there been a will to do so. Now almost in a hypochondriacal way, the minute the economy begins to flag the least little bit, the stops are pulled out in favor of expansion. This is true in the Federal Reserve as well as in the executive branch.

Here is a trivial example. In some years life insurance policies of veterans are paid out on their birthdays. That gives you a random distribution through the year. In other years, you will note that they are paid out early in the year. These are not accidents. I hesitate to call this sort of thing fine tuning. I sometimes think that Walter Heller is too gifted in the use of words and the creation of expressions. I mean too gifted for the good cause. But this is not fine tuning; it's merely an example of the new activism.

CURRENT ACTIVISMS

Now, let's take this particular year itself. I want to address our attention to it because I want to examine how dependent we are upon accurate forecasting.

I heard it said the other day at a private meeting within the government that the government forecast had been essentially right this last year. I found that an interesting and surprising statement — surprising because I think that the 1967 January figure given by the government was too optimistic. I even think that some of the analysts in the government at that moment, if asked qua scientist and having to bet their family fortune on it, would also have thought that it was a little bit too optimistic at the time. But, of course, it is not their private scientific forecast. It is part of a total picture and there is often a difference of opinion among the experts.

A very high official in the government, who is not an economist, told me that he felt in his bones that plant equipment expansion was going to increase by 11 percent. All of the surveys showed something very different. I told him he had better go see his orthopedist—if that was the case, the man was in trouble, in my judgment.

But, in any case, I think the government people were

high in terms of what happened. Yet they are now doing the new things which will help their wrong forecast from ending up too far wrong. Although I may turn out to be wrong, it does look to me now in April as if we are going to get through this year probably without having the National Bureau pull out the change in stationery for a recession. I don't say this on the basis of the foolish notion that the inventory adjustment is behind us. I don't see how there could yet have been enough time for any sizable adjustment to be behind us.

The release of highway funds I think is indicative of the government activistic policies that will lessen the chance of a recession. This has been done three times now. We mustn't overemphasize the announcement effects and the size of this sort of thing, but the increase in Vietnam spending that is on the way does bulk large. Note too the really surprising rate of expansion by the Federal Reserve of the money supply. I think all this is very likely to turn this thing around. It may, indeed, take us from the frying pan into the fire, and we may be soon worrying about the other problem of inflation as a result of this trigger-happy activism that I have been speaking about with such admiration.

Notice that it doesn't take such terribly accurate forecasting, if these are your weapons and this is your philosophy. In a sense the forecasts fulfill themselves because, one way or another, you are going to get by activism a better than 3-to-4 percent increase in money GNP.

I still do fault the January forecaster because I don't

think he forecast that he would be now doing these things in order to get his target. But if you judge him by the sum of the squared deviations from what he said would happen and what actually happens, after he has had another whack at the control mechanisms that are involved, I think his forecasting record will look better than it otherwise would be. God knows it's bad enough as it is. But my point is that with this kind of behavior you don't have to have all that accurate forecasting.

The difficulty is, and this is the weakness in my argument, many things do operate with a lag. If what our right hand does today had its effect upon the economy tomorrow, we would have limited need of accurate forecasting. If what our right hand does today has actions nine months from today and nothing along the way can change that action, then it's quite obvious that we must have some notion of what things are going to be like nine months from now.

GAY STAGNATIONISTS?

Now, to go back to the cyclical versus trend thinking. It was that kind of notion which I believe was in the minds of the people on my task force, of the Council of Economic Advisers, and of the new economists generally.

Professor Burns coined the expression for the new economists in April of 1961, the gay stagnationists. Once my textbook, by the way, said "rentier" rhymes with "gay," in *Time* fashion. A businessman who took a dim view of my economics orthodoxy said, "That's quite un-

fair." I said, "What's the matter with it? I didn't think
it was very funny but what's unfair about it?" He said,
"You know what I mean." I said, "No, I don't know
what you mean." He said, "Well, ask a psychologist
friend of yours what gay means." Well, I asked him and
I learned something. Now, when Professor Burns spoke
of the gay stagnationists, I doubt that there was any
innuendo intended in his remarks. But it did remind
me a little bit of the thinnest fat man in the world,
these stagnationists who are exuberant and enthusiastic.

Still, he had his difference of opinion in 1961. I know
that he disagreed on technical grounds with the gap concept, its operational measurement and the confidence
with which you could hold a view with respect to the
gap's size at that time. Nevertheless, the Council of
Economic Advisers in those days, Heller, Tobin, and
Gordon—it's like the Notre Dame football teams of
earlier years to mention the names of such giants—had
the notion that the gap was here, that it was large, and
that it was going to be there for some time and so the
expansionary things that they did at that time and that
needed to be done would not have to be quickly reversed.
One couldn't be cocksure of this, and there were argu-
able differences of opinion.

If I may go back to those times, there were people
from early in 1961 who were worried about the pace of
the advance and who counseled moderation of that pace.
This was before the Berlin Wall incident. This was before
quite a number of the tax changes that were subsequently

made. The Council was not of this cautious frame of mind. Even I thought they were overly optimistic. I expected Phillips curve problems by 1963. I am very happy for all of us that I was wrong and that we had from 1958 to 1964 stability in the wholesale price index and what today passes for moderation in the GNP deflator index and in the consumers' price index.

Yet I always felt that those who urged moderation were going to come into their time and that there would arrive a time when expansion would be overdone and when we ought to do something about it. I believed that the end of 1965 was that time.

Now, I know there are people who say that it was merely a question of the Federal Reserve going crazy in 1965 and of M increasing too fast. My interpretation is that it is all much more complicated; e.g., the Vietnam increase from the middle of 1965 and for the next three quarters was a colossal amount by any account. So you can have a GNP model to explain the exuberance of that period or you can have an M model: each will come to the same conclusion.

I thought that we were lucky in 1965-66 that that inflation looked to be of the demand-pull type, for demand-pull inflation requires macroeconomic therapy that is a matter of dosage. We should have had more macroeconomic fiscal restraints in early 1966. I don't know whether it can be judged by history that reliance on the wage-price guideposts was a factor in putting off reliance upon macroeconomic policy. I am inclined to doubt it; but, if it was a factor, then it is something which you must debit against the wage-price guideposts because, in my view, we did have too little restrictive fiscal policy. Thus I quite disagree, and have done so in rather bad-tempered terms, with Secretary Fowler's discussion on the Monday morning quarterbacks, which alleged that the government did exactly the right thing last year with respect to overall fiscal policy.

I am not sure but that by the last quarter of this year you will not want to have some contractionary dosage with respect to macroeconomic policy, which means something like the 6 percent surcharge. I counseled against it last New Year. I now [April, 1967] counsel against it for July 1st. But I cannot in conscience, on the basis of the evidence and the probabilities, say "Put it away for another 12 months; it won't be in season."

DISCUSSION

FIRST SESSION[1]

JOHN PIERSON, United Press International: Professor Burns, do you think that we are in a recession now or on the brink of one?

PROFESSOR BURNS: I see little basis for saying that we are now in a recession. That is the only answer I can give, if you mean by a recession what we at the National Bureau of Economic Research have over the years meant by a recession. We think of a recession as being a sustained decline in aggregate economic activity lasting at least six months. The economy has turned sluggish in recent months, but one cannot properly claim that a sustained decline has begun. Hence, it would be entirely premature to speak of our being in a recession.

It has been clear to me since last summer that we would be heading into a period of considerable sluggishness. But my powers of prediction have not been adequate to the task of judging whether the economy in 1967 would rise a little, move horizontally, or decline a little. That is a subtle distinction and I cannot do any better today.

I might note that there is more than one concept of a

recession. Thus the Japanese, and also some Europeans, consider any sharp retardation of growth as a recession. In terms of that concept of recession, the answer to your question is clearly that we are in one and have been for some time.

But, to return to the American concept, I am not ready to say that there has yet been an appreciable decline in aggregate economic activity, and I am certainly not prepared to say that we are likely to experience a sustained decline. After all, while there are many forces of weakness in the economy at present, you must not overlook the fact that government expenditures, at all levels, are rising very rapidly. Under such conditions, a significant decline in economic activity seems quite unlikely to me. On the other hand, it is plain that the boom in business capital investment has temporarily come to an end, and that a very sizable inventory adjustment must still take place. Such a correction takes time. While the optimists who believe that the inventory adjustment can be completed by mid-year may turn out to be right, historical experience is against them. Inventory adjustments of the magnitude that now face us have not been completed in the past in so short an interval.

PROFESSOR MELVILLE ULMER, University of Maryland: Professor Burns, I understood you to say that it is impossible to tell, at the present time, just how low a level of unemployment we can hope to reach through stimulating aggregate demand. I gather from you that we need more data in order to determine this. I wonder if you could tell us, since this is a very important question, just what data you think we could acquire that would let us know what is a legitimate goal in this.

PROFESSOR BURNS: As you phrase the question, I would have to say that unemployment could surely be brought down below 4 percent, that it could come down to 3 percent, or even to 2 percent, by a sufficiently rapid expansion of aggregate monetary demand. I don't think there can be any serious doubt about this. We proved it during World War I, we proved it again during World War II and during the Korean War, and other nations have proved it time and again during the postwar period.

The critical question, however, is this: how far is it safe to keep expanding aggregate demand when you have some concern not only for the unemployment that exists today, but also for the integrity of the nation's money and for the unemployment that may be here tomorrow? Statesmen must concern themselves with the welfare of the entire population and they must have some concern for the future as well as for today.

In handling this difficult problem, the most important body of statistics that we need, but do not yet have, is statistics on job vacancies. At present, we have data on the supply side of the labor market, but we lack data on the demand side. If we had comprehensive data on job vacancies and proceeded to match them with data on unemployment, we could tell at once whether aggregate demand is or is not sufficient—in principle—to make it possible for everyone who wanted to work to have a job.

For example, if job vacancies just equaled the number of unemployed, you would not have a deficiency in aggregate demand. You might still have a lot of unemployment, but then the problem would be to bring together somehow those who were unemployed with those who were seeking workers. This would require labor market techniques and policies, rather than an aggressively expansionist monetary and fiscal policy.

In view of what is now possible through the computer and telecommunication, we ought to have a system such that a workingman could walk into any employment office and within a matter of minutes find out about all the jobs suited to his requirements that are available within a radius of 25 miles, a radius of 50 miles, etc. Likewise, any employer ought to be able to locate quite promptly suitable employees within this or that geographic radius. We can't do that today, although it is technically a very easy problem. Hence there is a need to change institutions and habits of thought. The U.S. Employment Service used to be one of the stodgiest of the bureaucratic outfits in this wonderful city. Whether it still is or not, I do not know. But I have yet to see it develop the initiative and dynamism that are needed.

Moreover, while we are doing far more with training programs than we did only a few years ago, I don't think we are doing enough and I don't think we are doing it well enough. The vocational education program in this country is obsolete and needs to be overhauled to suit the nation's business and technological requirements.

To return to your question, I think we have a critical need of data on job vacancies to tell us whether and to what degree a deficiency of aggregate demand exists. With such data at hand, we would in practice find ourselves putting more emphasis on labor market policies than we have been doing; in other words, we would seek full employment through policies that would give us a little more protection against inflation.

There are many other statistical needs. Our wage statistics and our price indexes are not nearly precise enough to suit the needs of a full employment policy that is sensitive to the danger of inflation. Inventory statistics are neither prompt enough nor precise enough. And our estimates of the gross national product involve too much guesswork.

HARVEY SEGAL, *Washington Post*: Professor Burns, what would you do to reduce the destabilizing role of monetary policy? How, after your very lucid account tonight, would you improve it in the future?

PROFESSOR BURNS: Well, I think that it would be desirable for the Federal Reserve Board to keep the rate of change in bank credit more nearly stable than it has been accustomed to doing. The shifts are frequently more abrupt than they need to be.

Circumstances may, of course, arise when abrupt shifts in policy will be needed. Think of what the Labor government in England has done recently. That government was elected on the promise that it would put an end to the stop-and-go policy, but it had the bad luck of inheriting a serious balance-of-payments problem. At first, it hesitated to take bold steps to restrict the expansion of domestic demand which was the heart of the difficulty. Later, as the position of the pound continued to deteriorate, the Labor government shifted abruptly to orthodox policies—indeed, to far more orthodox financial policies than any Conservative had dared to suggest or perhaps even to dream of.

Circumstances like that can arise in any nation's life. However, they can often be avoided by responding more promptly to economic problems, instead of waiting for the crisis stage. I think that abrupt shifts by the Federal Reserve Board have been too frequent in our nation's history. Our monetary authorities, along with the rest of us, need to learn how to forecast better. In the absence of marked improvement in this respect, they need to recognize that oscillations of monetary policy may easily prove destabilizing.

HERBERT STEIN, Committee for Economic Development: My question is somewhat related to the previous one. At the end of your talk, you seemed quite optimistic about our learning from experience and complimentary about what had been learned in the last five or six years. But as I look over the body of the talk, I am not sure that this learning process has been a secular trend rather than a cyclical process. The Eisenhower Administration seems to have learned after 1958 that inflation was the great danger, that unemployment was transitory, and that what we needed was even bigger surpluses than had been achieved in 1956 and 1957. So they pursued that policy. They pursued it to extremes, stopped the inflation, left their successors with a huge full-employment surplus to work with. Then the successors learned that lesson. They learned that the large full-employment surplus was a drag on the economy, that the great danger was stagnation and that inflation was stopped. They pursued a policy to correct that. They ran that into the ground by 1965. That is what the learning consisted of—to exchange mistakes with their predecessors. So I am wondering just what your general reaction is to our secular learning processes as distinct from—

PROFESSOR BURNS: I agree with much of your comment. In fact, I tried to convey in my paper that what we learn from experience, we remember for a time and then, not infrequently, we forget again and repeat the old mistake. Economic policies themselves have a way of moving in cycles. For a time they are in tune with underlying conditions, but then a good policy is pushed beyond need or reason. This has been true too often, as you suggest.

And yet I see, or think I see, a gradual secular improvement in policymaking. To begin with, while mistakes in economic forecasting have certainly been made in recent years, no recent mistake in forecasting, or in policy based on forecasting, can compare with the blunder of January, 1949, when—with the nation already in a recession— President Truman came forward with a massive anti-inflation program. Forecasting is still a very imperfect art, but that kind of mistake has not been made recently and I think it unlikely that it will be made in the calculable future. Our factual information has been improving and we have become more skillful in using the information at our disposal.

We have also made advances in thinking about fiscal policy. Even the conservatives among us are less fearful of budgetary deficits than we were before. We recognize that a budgetary deficit for a year or two, or possibly a little longer, need not mean that inflation will result. This improved understanding of the role of governmental finances in our economy helped policymakers not only in the Kennedy-Johnson years, but also during some of the Eisenhower years. I think that this is a significant gain.

Not less important, the constructive role of businessmen and the influence of profits on the rate of innovation and investment are understood better today than they were in the 1930s or 1940s. Governmental policymakers have therefore become more mindful of the need to maintain a healthy state of business and investor confidence.

I think also that we have a better understanding today than we did 10 or 15 years ago of the large role that changes in the supply of money and credit have in our kind of economy.

So, while we keep taking some steps forward and some steps backward, we are making progress on balance. Our record is not nearly good enough, but if it is taken in the large and looked at fairly, it is an impressive record all the same. I expect that we will continue to make gradual improvements in our overall economic policymaking, although I sometimes wonder whether our policymakers are not overreaching their strength.

PROFESSOR HENRY BRIEFS, Georgetown University: Professor Burns, you covered the area very carefully and it is very difficult to find anything that you have not covered. There is only one point that I would like to ask you about and it is this. I think that one of the factors in the difficulties that we faced in 1966, looking back to 1965, was not only an underestimate of defense spending connected with Vietnam but, of equal importance, the impact of the defense spending on the economy. We get our figures from the national income budget when delivery is made which means at a time when inventories are being turned over and cash is being turned over the other way. So that we tend to neglect the lag of the impact in government spending on the demand for resources. It seems to me that this is one of the factors that was quite important in the misjudgment of the amount of inflation impact that the Vietnam War had on the economy. I would suggest that, in terms of policy, one would have to look at the second half of 1965 or, let's say, the fourth quarter, rather than early 1966 in order really to look at the inflation in its incipiency.

PROFESSOR BURNS: I certainly agree with your technical point that it is far more important to pay attention to defense orders and defense contracts, and their timing, than to defense expenditures as reported in the national income accounts. Those are interesting magnitudes, but as you point out, they have a tendency to lag.

Now, turning to the issues of policy, the proper time for governmental restraint was in 1965—in the late summer of 1965. After that, it was already late. Much of the criticism that has been leveled at the administration for not acting on taxes early in 1966 has missed this vital point. The basic mistake was made in 1965, not in 1966. And yet, as I tried to bring out in my paper, it was difficult in 1965, given the economic and political environment, to bring about the necessary measure of restraint. Therefore, those of us who have our feet on the ground cannot look forward to a world that will soon be free of instability or that will be recession-proof. Some kinds of mistakes are difficult to avoid.

PROFESSOR NATHAN A. BAILY, American University: I was interested, Dr. Burns, in your comment that, in effect, the government was asking the business firms and the labor unions to play a role that might be argued was really a governmental role. I could raise a whole series of questions, but I would like to ask one. What impact on this whole picture is coming from the increasing employment of economists by private business firms and, presumably, the increasing influence that the business economist is having on management decisions in business firms?

PROFESSOR BURNS: I think that the influence of

economists on the world of business is increasing tremendously. I think also that their influence, by and large, has been salutary.

PROFESSOR BAILY: Does it tend to make the business firm pursue its own economic interests regardless of Washington, as you imply, or does it make the business firm more effectively an agent of government?

PROFESSOR BURNS: With or without the aid of economists, businessmen generally pursue the interests of their stockholders, and that necessarily means that they also pursue the interests of their workers and their communities. Yet, much of what we hear from government people, and sometimes from businessmen, about the public responsibilities of business is just rhetoric. Who is an authority on the public interest? What do businessmen know about the public interest? How can they best act in the public interest? Government officials like to think that they are the authorities, but that is a little presumptuous on their part.

Businessmen are qualified by training and aptitude to manage resources—to expand markets, to lower costs, to seek out or create new opportunities for putting resources to more effective uses. When a businessman develops a new and superior product or brings down the cost of a shirt by a nickel or a cent, he is making a contribution to the public interest and one that we must never underestimate. That is the major function of businessmen in our society and we should not expect more of them than they are capable of doing. I sometimes wonder, as I listen to some of my business friends, whether they think they are running little Health, Education, and Welfare shops. The sums which they so generously contribute to colleges and so on are not their distinctive contribution. The government can do that too. Their real contribution is to put resources to increasingly effective uses, and this is something that the government is not especially good at. Of course, I like to see businessmen be good citizens. They should be. We need good corporate citizens just as we need good personal citizens. But the vital function of a businessman is to make a profit in the marketplace. In an economy characterized by keen competition, and ours is certainly that, profits are the critical test of how well a business serves the public.

To expect businessmen to act counter to their own interests is to expect them to give up the constructive role which they play in our society and to assume a role which they are not really capable of performing. It by no means follows, when a businessman does what some government official thinks is right in the sphere of prices, that he is really serving the public interest. Higher prices may be inconvenient to government officials, but they commonly serve the function of stimulating larger production of what the public demands. Moreover, it is naive to expect businessmen or trade union leaders to overlook their own interests and to do what this or that official happens to consider the public interest. That is a highway to illusions. What happens when government officials develop faith in the wage and price guidelines? Well, the government can then pursue an expansionist policy and trust that the trade union leaders and business executives will somehow see to it that inflation does not occur. This kind of illusion delays recognition of the need for corrective policies, and it postpones the taking of corrective policies.

MR. PIERSON: You said the Federal Reserve Board should avoid abrupt shifts in monetary policy. Do you think that the current shift toward easier money has been too abrupt?

PROFESSOR BURNS: Yes, I think that, as of today, the Federal Reserve Board is overdoing things. Looking at the record of February and March, it seems to me that the Federal Reserve Board is permitting bank credit to rise much too rapidly once again. However, this is a tentative judgment. When the figures for April are out, the record may look better. In any event, I fail to see the advantage of the recent sudden, sharp movements of bank credit. An abnormally high rate of increase is just that; it cannot be maintained, and this may bring trouble later.

SECOND   SESSION

LOUIS DOMBROWSKI, *Chicago Tribune*: Dr. Samuelson, what in your opinion is the future of the guideposts as to the economy, say next year or ten years from now?

DR. SAMUELSON: I think that the single number, like 3.2 percent which had a certain understandability because it was a single number, is dead.

It was not replaced by a new single number this year, and I think perhaps advisedly. I would hesitate to know what number to replace it by.

But I think the problem of incomes policy remains and something like guideposts philosophy and oratory plus the influence of government is going to be here if we meet ten years from now.

Take something like moral suasion of the Federal Reserve. I have been in economics now for about 30 years and I have heard that moral suasion is dead, and that it never was alive. But still you just can't seem to kill it off. In Canada and Great Britain where you have a few large banks, moral suasion is very, very important.

I think that it has considerable, if marginal, importance now in the U.S.A. and I think it is going to be more important in the mixed economy of the future than it is today. This means that the Federal Reserve is going to be less automatic and mechanical and standoffish and more directly communicative with the actors.

In that same sense, I think the wage-price guideposts are here to stay.

But the strong effect that the President can get when he loses his temper with the head of some large company, who is not at his public relations best in the incident, does dissipate itself. You can't keep repeating the rope trick by losing your temper and having confrontations on each new thing.

That part of it, I think, inevitably declines in importance.

MR. DOMBROWSKI: But do you think that they will essentially establish a new single number at some later date? Or from year to year?

DR. SAMUELSON: I doubt that a new number can be found which will be of lasting significance, namely good for a three or four-year period.

That raises the question whether we will have some kind of an ever-moving guidepost figure like the parity figure in agriculture.

Technically, the way the Council explained how it got its first figure—and it may later have regretted that it ever gave the explanation—was by taking a five-period moving average.

They didn't want the productivity of any one year.

They wanted something representative, so they took a five-period moving average.

Well, in the course of a five-period moving average, a year passes, you add a figure and you drop a figure. But sometimes you don't like the productivity of the year that you are adding, and sometimes you are losing a figure that you wanted very much, such as an early recovery period.

Still, if there are going to be numbers, I think it will probably have to go toward a *moving* set of numbers. I am not so sanguine of the political sex appeal of it when there will be a numbers game as against qualitative exhortation.

Of course, guideposts also can be periodic phenomena. We have right now in the United Kingdom a definite kind of a freeze. Since I have rejected the Galbraith argument that in times of peace these things work well on a permanent basis, you know that I don't think that the U.K. could live with that. But that it can gain some time to help bring its balance of payments into some sort of temporary equilibrium, I don't doubt.

My general view about selective controls—installment controls *and* such—is that they are very powerful. But they don't last, and therefore you want to keep them in reserve for those emergency periods rather than use them up.

It's like some new antibiotic, to which the germs will gradually develop resistance. You want to save it for an emergency and not use it on a common cold.

DONALD WEBSTER, Joint Economic Committee: You spoke of the possibilities of improving the Phillips curve. You said that during the 1960s the balance-of-payments problem and perhaps the unemployment of the Eisenhower years had this effect. How would you evaluate our training and retraining programs, the new programs, in contributing to this? That's the first part.

And the second part: Do you think that training programs, retraining programs, perhaps considerably expanded, could enable us to improve the Phillips curve sufficiently so that we could have an acceptable level of unemployment, perhaps 3.5 percent, and a reasonably stable price level? And without the guidelines, or guideposts?

DR. SAMUELSON: I think that training and manpower programs can help the Phillips curve, particularly with respect to the unemployment rates of young people. I should also have mentioned that one of the things that improves the Phillips curve is a long, steady expansion. I think that if you have been experiencing unemployment in a mixed economy of 8 to 10 percent for a decade or half a decade, it is quixotic to think that in any short period of time you can get unemployment down to 4 percent.

But a lot of the hard core of unemployment does melt, and I think that success in job expansion breeds success and gives you a better Phillips curve in some degree. I don't want to rehash the debate on structural unemployment, but by and large we know that the regional problem—the so-called West Virginia story—has been getting better all the time. I don't mean that West Virginia has been getting better, although I gather it has been getting a little bit better too. But what I mean is that West Virginia is the exception. CED, in a study of the two censuses, 1950 and 1960, found that on a state basis, on a regional basis, and on a metropolitan-district basis, we are getting an evening up of the amount of unemployment around the country and not a worsening of pockets of unemployment.

In summary, it seems to me plausible that the re-training side of the picture would help the Phillips curve. I haven't myself had the opportunity to review our recent experience with this, but I would think that this is a place where you can spend quite a lot of social resources with advantage.

I would welcome, though, learning what the actual experience has been. We do an awful lot of things socially, but don't scientifically follow through and see how it worked out. I remember when Bill Batt ran the Regional Development Program in the early Kennedy days. He didn't know at all how the certificates of necessity given in the Korean period for plants in distressed areas had worked out. Consider a plant that got a certificate of necessity with rapid amortization. Did that plant survive or did it only live as long as it had the subsidy?

Now, there should have been some way of keeping track of that. After all, Kennedy came in just seven years later, and if we spent all of that money on doing things, we ought to try to learn something from the experience.

HERBERT STEIN, Committee for Economic Development: I wish you would say a little more about your view of the Phillips curve in the long run. As I understand [University of Chicago Professor Milton] Friedman's argument, he essentially says that unemployment is a real phenomenon and it depends upon real characteristics of the economy, and the general change of the price level is not a real phenomenon and shouldn't be expected to affect unemployment aside from its transitional or unexpected changes. Now, what's wrong with that?

DR. SAMUELSON: I don't think unemployment is simply a real phenomenon. At least I don't think much follows from saying it is.

I particularly balked at the wording. I don't mean to be unkind, and am trying to be constructively critical. Let's take, for example—I don't know whether this is a realistic model, but it's not a wild model—a case where the Phillips curve is pretty good or pretty bad, but is definitely permanent and actually doesn't shift through time.

Now, in such a model changes in mere purchasing power, where you are on the Phillips curve, do change permanently the amount of unemployment.

We could argue in terms of plausible causal sequences and empirical behavior whether this particular model is relevant or whether it is worse than some particular inter-temporal model. But I cannot accept that anything necessarily follows from the fact that unemployment is a real thing and the price level is a money thing, that unemployment must therefore be unaffected by the degree of purchasing power.

I don't know whether I have been constructive. You have to be the judge of that.

PROFESSOR MELVILLE ULMER, University of Maryland: I believe you said that we might expect that the guidelines would gradually improve our Phillips curve as it induced business firms and labor unions to take a more moderate attitude towards price and wage increases.

I wonder whether, using the laboratory of the world and looking at Western Europe, you find any evidence of that in those countries, particularly since most of them have used the counterpart of guidelines for 10 or 20 years.

DR. SAMUELSON: The European experience is a very mixed one. I have here a study made for the Canadian Council that brings up to date and reviews incomes policy in different countries. The different European countries differ considerably in how bad their Phillips curves are. For a long time I envied Germany its Phillips curve, and I think I still do a little bit. Right now there is some unemployment in Germany developing for the first time. There is some slack in the economy and some slowdown.

I was just speaking to Professor Krelle from Bonn University, and was told that the labor unions there like to be respectable and fear that the man in the street is rather critical right now of wage demands.

The problem is that the union movement also feels that over a long period of time it can and should affect the relative distribution of income. As economic analysts we feel that it can do this only within narrow limits and over very long periods of time. What we don't want is for the struggle over the division of the pie to result in a paper increase in prices.

I don't know whether I'm being optimistic, but it seems to me that the union movement—and I speak of the rank and file as well as the leadership—is less interested now than in the 1950s in money increases that will be self-defeating because they can be expected to be followed by general price increases. This may be because unions are on the run. It may be because the kind of occupations which you can unionize are blue collar and northern and are in relative decline.

I have heard it said, but I do not have any experience, that in the Common Market there are not international unions across all six countries; the unions in each country, as the economies become more open, are quite conscious that they will lose employment of their people to the rest of the Common Market; and this therefore leads them to have more moderation in their wage increases.

To respond directly to your question, there have been some disappointments in the European experience. We used to point to the Netherlands. Here was a country where they really did things right. Jan Tinbergen on one famous occasion told the unions, "The nation can't afford a wage increase. Don't ask for a wage increase now. But I'll be watching, and when I think the country can afford one, I'll give you one." And, according to the tale, that's exactly the way it worked out: the unions held back; then after a while Tinbergen looked around and said, "Now you can have one," and everything worked very well.

Well, in the last three years, four years, wages have risen 37 percent in the Netherlands. A few years ago, although the governmental machinery had decided on a 6 percent wage increase, it turned out to be 12. Later they decided on a 9, and it turned out to be 17.

Fortunately they have such productivity miracles that when this happens to them, it doesn't ever seem to give *us* a balance-of-payments surplus. I say fortunately for them, and unfortunately for us.

This recent experience goes back to the fact that guidelines are not a substitute for macroeconomic policy. They were running the system so tight that the thing broke of its own accord, because when they succeeded in holding wages down in the Netherlands, Dutch workers began to go to Germany. And what is the point of getting Spaniards and Greeks and Moroccans into the Netherlands, as they were doing, only to be losing your own workers? When labor markets get very tight, the interest of the employer coincides with that of the worker and the union; firms want wages raised in the attempt to attract workers from elsewhere. Europe has had a problem which we haven't had in any degree yet, the problem of so-called "wage drift." In the United States, by and large, except for piece rates, the negotiated minimum wage rate is also the maximum wage. But that isn't true in the over-full-employment countries.

Without incomes policy, maybe it would have been a lot worse there than that. I'm not sure.

NORMAN TURE, National Bureau of Economic Research: Paul, may I put an illustration to you? Let's take two economies, A and B, that are identical in every respect except with respect to the use of wage-price guideposts. One does use the guideposts in order to maintain full employment and avoid the price creep. The other doesn't. It eschews the use of them and allows the price creep to go on. Isn't it likely that after a number of years the distribution of resources and distribution of income will differ between the two countries? And if that is likely, what is the a priori basis for the assessment that one is better off than the other?

DR. SAMUELSON: Well, let me answer the second part of the question first. I would say that if you had a closed economy with no international trade relationships, the mild creeping inflation of the sort that you posit, which isn't so certain that everybody can count on it every year but still averages out on the up side, is a possible way of life.

In an open system, it seems to me that you cannot have, with fixed exchange rates, one economy having a stronger price creep over a long period of time than the other. Being something of a pessimist in this regard, I long thought that our problem is not to have stable prices but to have prices and wages and productivity such that our increase is not greater than that abroad. In fact, because, in my opinion the dollar was a little bit overvalued earlier, costs here had to rise a little bit less over the decade than costs abroad.

So my answer to you would be that, except for the differences that I'll discuss in answer to your first question, I don't see why you couldn't go on except for the balance-of-payments problem. I think it's rather lucky that we are all mixed economies together. We can't *all* run deficits because we each act like a mixed economy. All we have to do is act about as mixed up as other economies, and we probably won't have to worry about the balance of payments.

Now, on the guideposts, what is the difference between an economy with guideposts working and one with open inflation? I am not thinking of a successful guideposts policy as one which really has a large measure of suppressed inflation. If you have an economy in which the prices are held down, then prices aren't operative, you can't buy anything at those prices. That's the classical case of suppressed inflation. Under it you will get certain redistribution effects. But you will also get a lot of *deadweight* effects. So I would expect that the country with a mild amount of open inflation is better off than one with suppressed inflation of that sort.

The guidepost philosophy, where it applies—that is, in the realm of the 500 largest corporations and in the collective bargaining sphere, and in the general attitude of employers and workers in the nonunionized sector— if it works, it seems to me, does work with prices still clearing markets.

PROFESSOR TURE: That wasn't the point I was raising.

DR. SAMUELSON: So I don't see that there would be any great distributional differences.

PROFESSOR TURE: I was not talking about the suppressed inflation case at all. I was simply assuming that, by virtue of the fact that the allocative mechanism has got to be a little bit different where an effective guideposts policy is operating than in one which would allow prices to move and in general to creep upward. After some period of time the composition of activity in that economy, the first economy, is likely to differ from that of the second. The question that I raise with you is: Why, on a priori grounds, should one assume that that shift in resource utilization and the consequent shift in the allocations of incomes is preferable on any welfare basis than that creep in inflation?

DR. SAMUELSON: Yes. And I have been trying to respond to you. I don't respond with confidence but this is my hypothesis: where the guideposts are working, the allocative mechanism *is not very different,* except in one respect; namely, that we don't have the instability of the general price level.

In other words, I think that relative prices would be very much the same. An economist who studied the role of supply and demand schedules industry by industry would find them to be allocating resources in about the same way. It is the basis of the quantity theory of money and of much in macroeconomics that has never been seriously disputed that the absolute price level makes no great difference in the long run.

It doesn't help you much just to be changing your general price tags all the time. Hopefully a successful incomes policy will keep the price level from soaring unnecessarily.

PROFESSOR TURE: No, the case is not of soaring price levels but of creeping price levels.

DR. SAMUELSON: That's right. I think that considerable argument can be found that when you have a creeping price level that is foreseen, the distorting effects or the changing effects of allocation are not so great. For example, the interest rate gets built into it, some allowance for the rate of price change too. It is not true, for example, that only the holders of common stock are protected. Over time, bonds are renegotiated and other people also get protected. The substantive difference that remains is that the average real cash balance wouldn't be quite the same, as has been commented on by writers on monetary theory, but it seems to me this is a secondary effect.

ROBERT WILLIAMS, *Forbes* Magazine: Dr. Samuelson, I understand that the guideposts may have overlooked the process by which we can have a rise in the total labor cost nationally without individual rises in wage rates in certain industries through the migration factor, as workers move from lower paying industries or jobs into higher paying jobs, which has happened in the last year or so. My question is this: First, did the guideposts overlook this migration factor? And, secondly, can they, in the future, be modified so that they would include this?

DR. SAMUELSON: You are speaking now of the problem of upgrading, that every job could keep the same wage but, as you shifted the mix towards the higher paid jobs, you would get a change in average wages paid.

MR. WILLIAMS: Yes. Walter Heller mentioned in his letter this was a surprising thing, he thought, to many people this year. Even without higher settlements there would still be a higher cost.

DR. SAMUELSON: I think what we need to try to distinguish in our own minds is to decide whether this is a spurious effect or a real effect. If the same man doing the same work is reclassified as a higher paid worker then that's a hidden wage increase. But if, in fact, a man is moving from a low productivity function to a high productivity function, that is a true productivity improvement.

MR. WILLIAMS: Let's say the worker is just moving

from the rural area to the urban area to take a higher paying job.

DR. SAMUELSON: Yes, but if he is actually producing a higher real output, that would show in the calculation. You have to decide which of these effects you think it is.

Now, I think, as you get into fiats which actually hold wages down by law, you will encounter a spurious getting around the law by reclassification. The prime rate in banks, for example, can stay very sticky. If you don't qualify any more for the prime rate when money gets tight, that's a spurious difference.

I can't answer whether the original productivity figures of the Council sufficiently allowed for the fact that you spoke of. I think that their figures would have picked up the normal upgrading that goes on through time in their base period and that's all.

I didn't mention one of the things that would interest labor most about this year. Labor can feel that last year it got cheated because of the guideposts philosophy. Let's assume that labor got a wage increase not too much more than 3.2 percent.

That goal was premised upon reasonable stability of the consumer price index, defined either as a zero increase in the price index or the one-and-a-quarter percent increase in the consumer price index which would be typical of the earlier part of the 1960s. In fact, in 1966 we had a three-and-a-half percent increase in consumer prices—at least 2 percent more than that. So some could argue that they should have had, just for equity, since the guideposts didn't work, 5.7 percent wage increases!

I think there is some sympathy with that view in government: namely, that 1967 could, in equity, be a year of catching up; and for this year alone labor could get more than the productivity guideposts in order to make up for last year. What they didn't want to do was to give their blessing to escalation because they were afraid they'd get this catching up plus escalation in three-year contracts.

I think that if you have one year catching up and price-level escalation but no excessive improvement term in each year of three-year contracts, a good deal could be said in equity for that. It won't lead perhaps to stable prices but maybe we've given up on that because, in my opinion, we didn't have last year the proper macroeconomic dosage policy. I think last year we should have had early in the year a tighter fiscal policy, and shared restraints on the part of both monetary and fiscal policies.

PROFESSOR HENRY MANNE, George Washington University Law School: You seem to attach considerable significance to the possibility of effectively using moral suasion on the directors of the 500 largest corporations. Yet that seems to raise a number of difficult questions.

You offered us some evidence of what directors say they do about prices and yet, when the pressure is really on, this theory suggests that all of these individuals must trust each other, that none will break it, that the usual experience with cartels wouldn't be repeated here, that they won't lower quality as a way of raising prices. Even assuming that the whole system could be made to work, don't you still just wind up with a shift of resources to smaller companies not included in the 500 who in turn will, I presume, raise their prices?

DR. SAMUELSON: Well, now, I don't recognize that it takes the collusion of a tight cartel. All, it seems to me, it takes is a way of life that's shared, a shared consensus of our values. We are all members of society. We behave in certain ways, including such things as reporting truthfully to stockholders. If you have any experience with some other countries, you know how surprising it is that stockholders are told the truth about their company. I think that's all that is required.

Now, the question is whether the 500 largest corporations are constitutional monarchs who will be displaced the minute they begin to show some social consciousness. I go back now. This is related to the question from Norman Ture. It seems to me that, if the guideposts had the successful purpose of giving us a better Phillips curve so that we live with three-and-a-half percent unemployment as being consistent with reasonable overall price stability instead of 4 percent, it is not clear to me that the 500 largest corporations are doing something uneconomical, giving away something and, therefore, that somebody outside of the system can take a whack at them.

It merely seems to me that we are then just not all raising the balloon together in a self-defeating way.

PROFESSOR MANNE: Then you have made it in their self-interest to act in this way and no moral suasion is necessary.

DR. SAMUELSON: It is in their self-interest in this sense. Suppose you had Kant's categorical imperative and they were asked as a collective group: under this common rule are you all better off than under a different common rule? I think the answer is yes. But if you asked if 499 out of the 500 were behaving in this way it would be to the interest of the 500th to do so, then because they are in quasi-competitive relationships to each other and because their competitive relationship to each other is much greater than to the rest of small industry, I think it might still be in their interest.

PROFESSOR MANNE: Even that assumes that over a period of time there won't be a shift of resources to smaller businesses.

DR. SAMUELSON: I do think that the larger the business the more honest it is. It is not always true that honesty is the most profitable policy. So adherence to law and order, including the new kind of law and order of the mixed economy, is like a hidden tax on the largest business.

Now, to this degree, we do move things out of large business. But when I look at that result and stand off at a distance, there is just enough of old Judge Brandeis in me to think that this is not the worst situation in the world. Besides, it couldn't happen to a nicer bunch of guys.

PROFESSOR MANNE: But that's something you know as a judge and not as an economist.

DR. SAMUELSON: Certainly. What I was saying has something to do with my social welfare function and isn't technical economics.

But industrial statesmanship is one of the prices that could be paid. I also believe that to achieve the economies which exist in the large corporations, their size is a help. You can't get perfect substitutes for them elsewhere. If you could, I doubt that there would be any problem. If you had laissez faire reproducing atomistic competition, you probably wouldn't have a bad Phillips curve problem to begin with.

RICHARD LURITO, Georgetown University: Professor Samuelson, would you comment on the following possible argument: Because we have not walked along the ceiling for any great length of time, the trade-off between unemployment and price rise and sustained full employment may not be as bad as statistical estimates have suggested.

DR. SAMUELSON: I thought I did comment on that in connection with the question that I was asked about manpower; namely, that successful maintenance of a long expansion itself gives you a better Phillips curve. I don't know of any mixed economy that can go from a very high level of unemployment in a short period of time to a lower level.

Our memories are very short, but I can remember *Fortune* magazine in the immediate postwar period saying that we would need 7 million unemployed in the American system, just for normal lubrication of the joints. Now, I don't think that they were necessarily wrong when they wrote that. They were thinking of how much the unemployment had been in the 1930s and didn't know what the postwar was going to be like or that we would be able to work our way to lower levels.

I have always hoped that, after the proximate goal of 4 percent unemployment was reached, and I don't mean has been collided with, that you could push down below it—both by manpower and other policies but also just from people moving around, as they will under the pull of opportunity. So I hope I have commented on that quotation. Who was the quotation from, by the way?

MR. LURITO: I just made it up.

DR. SAMUELSON: Oh. That's like the fact that for many years the most colorful gown in the Harvard Processional was old Professor Albert Bushnell Hart's. Somebody once asked him, "Professor Hart, which Chinese university did you get that degree from?" He replied, "Oh, that's not from a Chinese university; it's just a mandarin kimono I saw once and liked."

THIRD SESSION

HARVEY SEGAL, *Washington Post:* I would like to address my question to Professor Samuelson. I was a little disturbed by the point that he made about it not being terribly necessary to forecast accurately. I wondered if he would care to comment about what I consider to be the tense period of uncertainty between, let's say, April and September, 1966, when it seems to me, although I can't prove it, that many of the administration economists missed a turning point, at least in the rate of GNP growth.

Certainly one's forecast determined one's position on whether or not to ask for a tax increase and it certainly must have had something to do with the unfortunate suspension of the investment tax credit in October.

DR. SAMUELSON: I would like to ask for clarification. Is it your implication that the economy from April to September of last year grew faster than had been forecast?

MR. SEGAL: No, I think that the rate was slowing down but I'm not sure that the forecasters or at least many of them were correct.

DR. SAMUELSON: Now, if I understood Secretary Fowler correctly, he took some credit to himself for having, in the face of experts outside of the government, noted the lessening of need for a tax increase after April and he would consider this an advantage on his side. I must confess that the first quarter of the year was stronger than I had expected. And I did expect a further continuation of that, not myself foreseeing the full slowing down that happened.

If you ask why, in the face of some slowing down, there was the suspension of the investment tax credit, there are a couple of factors to explain this:

One very important one was the desire to change the mix. The tight money was hurting very much. Ex-Presidents of the United States don't count for very much in American history, but sometimes when they speak and there is a resonant environment they are listened to. When Truman spoke from Independence, Missouri, and said, "Look, you're killing the country with tight money," I think that this was the last straw.

Behind the scenes, of course, when the Mellon Bank unloaded its municipals for whatever they would bring, there was what was called a near-crisis in the money market. I think that too gave rise to the determination to suspend the investment tax credit.

I don't suppose we have to blame, if that is what the economic historians of the future will do, Secretary Fowler or Assistant Secretary Surrey for the suspension because, to me, they gave all the signs of men who didn't want to suspend it. They had argued forcibly before Congress just before the event that it couldn't be done and gave all the reasons that it couldn't be done; so I didn't envy them the task of explaining how they were going to do what couldn't be done. I think it was a decision reached elsewhere.

Now, I am not persuaded that the suspension was a mistake. I admit that, if I had come out a month later with a recommendation that it be restored I could hardly have considered myself covered with glory for having urged its suspension.

You may ask: What's the difference between four months and one month? Well, it's not enough to be comfortable but I do think that the investment tax credit had for its purpose the lessening of the queues which were taking place in the machinery industries. We know from the Rinfret Survey which was taken at the same time, and which anticipated rather accurately the results of later official surveys, that there already was some decrease in the rate of increase of the plant and equipment spending.

So I think the change in mix was the motivation. It wasn't the government's being misled in thinking that in September the rate of growth of the GNP was fully as intense as it had been in the first quarter. For one thing, automobiles are always a bellweather, being probably given more importance than their actual quantitative importance in the GNP. And autos had definitely signaled a lessening of inflationary expansion and pressure after the first quarter, as I remember their sales.

PROFESSOR DUDLEY DILLARD, University of Maryland: For Professor Burns: Professor Samuelson has defended the guideposts essentially in terms that it makes for a better Phillips curve, that is, that we can push unemployment down further with the same price rise. Do you agree or do you basically disagree with this position?

PROFESSOR BURNS: Let me try to answer your question briefly.

I believe that the effect of the guideposts is likely to be quite small as a rule in our kind of economy, and I believe that it has in fact been quite small during the period since 1962. Possibly, the effect was for a while in Professor Samuelson's direction, but that is uncertain. In any event, and to repeat, the net effect of our price and wage guidelines appears to have been slight.

The second point that I would make is that the Phillips curve, as customarily used, merely records short-run responses and this can be quite misleading. I have no doubt at all that, even when unemployment is already moderately low, an aggressively expansionist policy can reduce the level of unemployment in the short run still further. What troubles me is that in the process of doing that you are likely to stir up inflationary pressures and create other imbalances in the economy. Therefore, in the course of reducing unemployment aggressively today, you may release forces that will enlarge unemployment tomorrow.

I think Professor Samuelson would grant this point, though he would perhaps argue that there is still a net gain. Whether that is so or not, I don't think that either he or I could answer categorically in the present state of knowledge.

PROFESSOR C. LOWELL HARRISS, Columbia University: Professor Samuelson, I did not have the privilege of hearing you last week. In regard to the guideposts, as I understood Professor Tobin at the 20th anniversary meeting last year, he said that one purpose the guideposts were to serve when they were formulated in January, 1962, was to guide government procurement, try to set standards for federal agencies in negotiating with defense, space, and other contractors.

Federal spending has been rising at a very rapid rate. In terms of 1966 dollars, the per capita federal expenditure next year will be about $200 per capita higher than it was ten years ago.

Now, do you have any impression whether the administration tried seriously to use the guideposts in their own contract negotiations?

DR. SAMUELSON: I don't have any knowledge on that subject. I would point out one related point but working in the deflationary direction. Because the government is a very important buyer, it has what Professor Galbraith might call countervailing power; it has sometimes used that power or the threat of that power to put some punch behind its exhortation.

For example, it is believed by business that, if you get

into a fracas with the government—let's say you are the oligopolist in the millinium industry who breaks the line and raises prices—that the word may go out to all of the Quartermasters, "When in doubt, when there is a tie, don't give the order to this fellow, give it to the other fellow."

It is not so important that it be true as that it be believed. I have heard some testimony of businessmen that they not only feel crucified before the bar of public opinion when dressed down by the President, but also that their own employees get penalized at a future date. Hence, they are a little more agreeable in playing ball.

We have seen government restraining pressure on prices with respect to stockpile behavior. Sometimes, if you have a stockpile, it's a good thing to get rid of it on a rising market; but sometimes when things are really scarce, that's when you really need the stockpile and you can't afford to use it to put out inflationary fires.

PROFESSOR HENRY BRIEFS, Georgetown University: The discussion about the guideposts seem to me to have two Achilles' heels that are not properly taken into account in this discussion. One is institutional and one is statistical.

Let me start with the statistical. As far as I know, the only really solid evidence of a statistical nature that argues for the general effectiveness of the wage guidepost is the George Perry study of wage determination. The difficulty with his econometric wage function is that once you get beyond the late 1950s that relationship breaks down progressively. As you add years and extend the experience, the coefficients become unstable; you get negative signs where there should be positive signs. Perry's relationship just doesn't seem to hold together.

In other words, we don't at this stage have a viable statistical test of the effectiveness of the wage guidepost, even in the manufacturing sector.

We have been doing a considerable amount of research on econometric wage functions at Georgetown University and we have developed some alternative models. The results seem to be that there is no general evidence for the effectiveness of the wage guidepost.

My second problem is that the guideposts, institutionally, are aimed at manufacturing and construction. A good deal of the long-term pressure on prices, however, comes from the service sector. If you get productivity gains of 1.5 percent over the long haul, according to Victor Fuchs, or maybe a little more in the recent period, you are going to get some inflationary pressure unless it is fully offset in manufacturing.

So the guidepost approach really requires that manufacturing prices must decline continuously and substantially over time in order to offset the increases in service prices. Given the wage determination process in manufacturing under existing institutions, is it reasonable to expect the requisite moderation in the rate of wage advance? Furthermore, how are you going to get after the fellows in the service and other sectors who may also be causing a good deal of long-term pressure on prices? The guideposts theory is that there are identifiable conglomerates of power in manufacturing and construction and you can bring pressure to bear on them. But, if that is only one source of the inflation, the guideposts are not an effective instrument to deal with the problem. It seems to me that, referring to the guideposts and then arguing, as Professor Samuelson has done, that we are now in a position to pursue a more expansionist monetary and fiscal policy rests on rather shaky ground.

DR. SAMUELSON: First, with respect to the George Perry analysis, I will remind you what that seems to show. His is a typical statistical study trying to predict wage changes from variables such as the existing amount of unemployment, the existing amount of profits in industry, the past amount of unemployment, the rates of change in those variables, and so forth.

It is my understanding that the Perry equations were based on pre-1963 data. When applied to post-1962 data, the equations predict higher wage increases than actually took place in the guidepost period.

What George Perry's equation shows quite a number of other similar studies have also shown. The usual argument goes, "Yes, the previous relationship does go haywire and it develops a residual; it is precisely the presence of the guideposts that is inferred by this residual. Guideposts explain the wage moderation."

If I understand you, you are saying something more

than that, that after you put in the guideposts as an explanatory dummy variable in the multiple regression, you then get in your internal estimation of the coefficients all kinds of haywire behavior.

Is that right?

PROFESSOR BRIEFS: It's that plus the fact that it ceases to overestimate the wage change.

DR. SAMUELSON: Yes, but that's the point of the demonstration, that Perry's equation without the guideposts doesn't estimate the wage increase and that, ergo, it's the presence of the guideposts that explains the moderation.

Now, if there is that other factor of signs of coefficients going haywire, then I have learned something here tonight.

On the question of service price increase, I don't think that there is anything spurious or illegitimate about increase in the price of services, provided that in the service area supply and demand is being cleared and there is no cost-push problem—as e.g., that it is actually the increase in demand for medical services that is bidding up the price of doctors in terms of supply. It certainly is true that, if services represent an industry with low productivity (as we measure it) and are an increasingly large part of the total picture, then the average productivity, which determines the average wage that we all can get, grows that much slower.

Does this mean that in your opinion the 3.2 percent

figure was not properly estimated, taking account of the service sector of the economy? Alvin Hansen before the Joint Economic Committee made an opposite point.

He said that taking the government's own figure, and considering there has always been a 1 percent increase in consumers' prices, then, in fact, a 4 percent figure is more justifiable for the allowable wage increase; if labor had gotten only the 3.2 percent, it would have continued to be cheated because of the 1 percent upward drift in the consumers' price index. I thought he must be wrong and that he hadn't really looked carefully at the figures, that these smart fellows in Washington would have a ready answer. But when I tried it out on a couple of them, they said, "Well, the kid's got a point there."

If his point is right about 4 percent, then the point about less than 3.2 percent can't at the same time be right. I think that there is room for more expository research in this particular area, particularly if you are going to play the numbers game and attach a great deal of importance to any particular number.

Can the economy as a whole justify a 4 percent increase, or, as your remarks seem to suggest, taking account of services, less than 3.2 percent over some extended period of time?

PROFESSOR BURNS: Let me say a word or two about Professor Perry's analysis, as I understand it. The book itself deals with data which stop, I think, in 1963. Therefore, Perry's analysis as such hardly tells you very much about the effectiveness of the guidelines. As you may recall, the guidelines were first proclaimed in January, 1962.

Furthermore, as I understand Professor Perry's analysis, he seeks to show what the rate of increase in wages would be, given the rate of unemployment, given the level of profits, etc. Now, there is another factor that I have always felt is of very considerable importance in wage determination, and that is how long a given level of unemployment has existed. I don't think this factor of duration is taken account of in Professor Perry's equations.

My recollection of Perry's analysis may be wrong and, if so, I would like to be corrected.

DR. SAMUELSON: May I say that I did comment on that last time and suggested that the only thing—the thing which is different in the post-1963 experience can't be said to be just the presence of the guideposts. There is, for example, the increased international trade pressure, which is not in his equations, and there is a possible factor along the lines of what Arthur Burns mentioned, which I mentioned earlier; namely, the legacy of the Eisenhower years of a sluggish economy with high unemployment whose effects might be expected to be felt for some period thereafter. Also, economists such as Simler and Tella can explain the Perry post-1962 residual by hypothesizing a hidden amount of unemployment because of the failure of marginal workers to enter the labor force when job opportunities were weak in the 1959-64 period.

Perry has a more recent different bit of evidence that guideposts may have been influential. He got experts to divide industries into the category of those in the public eye and those not. Then he looked to see whether wage increases had actually been more modest than might have been expected in those industries in the public eye and subject to guidepost influence. He did find unusually modest wage increases there.

PROFESSOR JOHN KENDRICKS, George Washington University: I would like first to make one comment, and then a question for Professor Samuelson.

My first comment is to take issue with Professor Hansen's comment, because I don't think the upward drift in the consumer price index is something independent of the change in wage rates which was going on.

I think it is agreed that the 3 percent or so increase in average wage rates is inflationary. In other words, a 3.2 percent guidepost I believe overstates the average increase you could get in wage rates in particular occupational groups consistent with a stable price level. The reason is that 3.2 is the average annual increase in real private product per man-hour, actually due to shifts of man-hours from lower paying to higher paying occupations generally. Part of this 3.2 was captured through these shifts, upwards of 1 percent.

A true non-inflationary wage increase is closer to, say, 2.5 percent, than to 3.2. This is a minor matter. I think we would all be delighted if wage rate increases were held to 3.2 and we would take the 1 percent inflation if we could be assured of so moderate a result.

The question I would like to address to Professor Samuelson is: Assuming that the guideposts have to be promulgated again more forcefully in the coming year, assuming success of expansionist policies that are being inaugurated at the present time, what modifications would he suggest in the guidepost formulation, particularly to meet the objections of so many people, as reflected in the Chicago conference of last year, the objections with respect to equity of the guideposts? The people who are the business managers who have social conscience and try to conform are penalized relative to those who don't, which also leads to some distortion in allocation of resources, as Milton Friedman points out. I am just wondering what modifications might be made, particularly to hit this problem of equity.

DR. SAMUELSON: I set up the hypothesis tentatively that the guideposts' only efficacy would be in the realm of the 500 largest corporations, and that by and large these compete with each other. Admittedly, over a period of time there could be some attrition in their position, if they take a socially conscious view—and I argued that they do have some leeway under our present degree of competition to take such a social view.

I argued that, in a sense, this is a tax on them. It means that a certain advantage spills over to small business which doesn't take that view; in a certain sense, it is a tax on the efficiency of the system, because these big fellows are probably efficient people.

But, I said then, that there was enough of old Justice Brandeis in me to think that it couldn't happen to a nicer bunch of fellows; that there was something to be said for keeping the system open; and that they can afford a little more weight in the horse race of life.

However, you could get to the point where, like all things, you are putting too heavy a handicap on the jockey who is riding this particular horse. At that point I would begin to ease up.

It is not all that clear that the guideposts are so successful that large corporations are carrying this tremendously heavy weight. I say this more in sorrow than in anger.

DANIEL EDWARDS, Joint Economic Committee: A question for both Burns and Samuelson. The Joint Economic Committee this week is holding hearings on post-Vietnam planning. The administration has admitted that, if Vietnam hostilities ceased tonight, the administration does not have contingency plans to put into effect tomorrow morning. I am wondering about the massive tax cut you recommended for after Korea.

In December, 1961, [Federal Reserve Board] Chairman Martin came up on the Hill and stated that the tax decrease that the administration was discussing would have to be financed out of real savings. The Federal Reserve Board shifted into a policy of rather significant restraint in the beginning of 1962. Some economists at the Board suggested that this restraint would lead to the largest stock market break since 1929 and it would lead to very poor performance in GNP.

Mr. [James] Tobin, in the Annual Report of the Council of Economic Advisers, indicated that there would be certain target values for money and liquid assets which would have to be provided in order to finance the target GNP for 1962. These values were not achieved. The administration did not follow the same policy with the Federal Reserve Board at that time that it did with the steel industry; it did not say anything publicly about monetary policy. Mr. Martin was much more aggressive in the 1950s in killing the dragon of inflation.

I am wondering if we had gotten a tax decrease, a massive one after Korea, if Mr. Martin would have emasculated this cut completely? Or, what are you assuming about the mix of fiscal-monetary policy?

DR. SAMUELSON: I thought it was idiocy, when we were proposing a massive tax decrease, for Mr. Martin to succeed in doing what he occasionally said he would and which was being urged upon us by many bankers, namely, to have it all come out of saving, or whatever the expression was. It was explained at that time this was necessary to appease the foreign bankers, the Gnomes of Zurich, who were concerned about our balance of payments, and who apparently didn't want us really to get any benefit from the tax cut.

To run a massive deficit, only to have it offset by a tight monetary policy, would have been bad for growth and nonexpansionary on total aggregates, if really contemplated. But I always felt at the time that Mr. Martin didn't understand what he was talking about, and that kept me from being very scared that it would come to pass.

MR. EDWARDS: Just look at what the Federal Reserve Board did in 1962 and, if you want, just look at the record of growth in this decade. The growth records for 1962 and 1966 are quite comparable. These are the two years that you get a departure in economic growth and reductions in the reserves available for private demand deposits on a quarterly basis.

DR. SAMUELSON: I don't think that, as grown men, we ought to spend our time relating the rate of change of money and of national income for past periods. Professor James Tobin has taken a new fresh look at all of the data and it is all practically pure noise.

The notion that anybody has demonstrated that you take the current rate of change of the money supply and the current rate of change of GNP and get a good prediction is ridiculous. You get a terrible scatter.

Even if you take past rates of change of the money supply and current changes of GNP, only by selective talk about incidents do you get a good fit. You do not get a good overall fit, as measured by correlation coefficients of say $+.8$.

If you take the models that were proposed by the proponents of this sort of simple money model, let's say in

1962, and apply them to subsequent times, they turn out just terrible in their predictions.

Or consider the rate of change of the money supply as a National Bureau leading indicator. The recent study of Geoffrey Moore and Julius Shiskin has rated each of the indicators in terms of their consistency and so forth. Shiskin told me just last week that the rate of change of the money supply was a pretty good indicator, not the best, but a pretty good one. However, he said, in the postwar period it has deteriorated considerably.

So it is ironical that precisely in the postwar period we hear about the crimes of the Federal Reserve of omission and commission. To me that's rhetoric. It has not yet been backed up by solid scientific research, and I have no reason to think that it can be. In fact, here is a view that reminds me of generals who win every battle but never have any territory solidly behind them.

NORMAN TURE, National Bureau of Economic Research: Paul, may I answer that objection just for a moment?

DR. SAMUELSON: Yes.

PROFESSOR TURE: It was, was it not, what the Federal Reserve Board did beginning last spring and leading up to the end of last summer that made it necessary for the administration to propose and to ram through the suspension of the investment credit and accelerated depression, which made it necessary for them to use a highly selective and very particularistic kind of tax device to correct deficiencies that were developing in the money market?

DR. SAMUELSON: I suggested something like that earlier this evening.

PROFESSOR TURE: I don't know why it's inconsequential then—to back Dan up—on the basis of the kind of observation you made a moment ago to write off what the Federal Reserve Board does.

DR. SAMUELSON: I don't. Money is one of the variables in my system, but to show that money matters is not to show that money *alone* matters, and that's what the modern debate unfortunately has degenerated into. It just turns out that when you examine the variables that you can't vindicate that monistic-money position, at least you can't in most counties in the country.

PROFESSOR BURNS: If I may, I would like to make an historical point.

Professor Samuelson suggested that we should have had a massive tax cut after the Korean War. Let me recall a few facts. First, in January, 1954, the excess profits tax went off. Second, the individual income tax was lowered, on the average, by 10 percent at the same time. Third, some excises were reduced in the spring of 1954. Fourth, the Revenue Act of 1954 provided for faster depreciation and futher lowered taxes.

Thus, in all, we had rather substantial tax reductions after the Korean War. My recollection is that the net tax reduction, after allowing for the increase in social security contributions, came to something more than $6 billion. Whether that is massive or not is a matter of opinion. It is worth noting, however, that the tax reduction of 1954 was not very different from the tax reduction of 1964 once account is taken of the size of the economy in these two years.

Now, going beyond the facts, I want to express a judgment. If we had had a larger tax reduction in 1954 than we did have, I am afraid that we would have had a still larger degree of inflation in the troublesome years 1956 and 1957.

DR. SAMUELSON: I think that I really ought to agree in part with that. I am now recalling the timing: The sluggishness that one was concerned about, I think, was in the last part of the 1950s. We should have been prepared, as Japan and some other countries have done, to have a succession of tax reductions.

It wasn't necessary to guess the long-term tax-cut dosage in 1953 when the hostilities ceased. Still I would have liked to have had the 1954 recession a bit lighter than it was. I don't think it was necessary for therapeutic purposes to have had all that we had then. But I do recall that 1955 and 1956 were years of upswing in the price level, partly of the demand-pull character; and I have to recall that 1957-58 showed disquieting cost-push behavior. With a more massive 1953 tax cut, we would have then been in the dilemma we are discussing tonight in a very marked way.

We are luckier in this decade. Aside from patting ourselves on the back as being smarter, of which there has been plenty of evidence, we actually are luckier: Productivity has done a lot better, and it couldn't have been counted upon to have done so; contrariwise productivity was just unfortunately bad in the 1957 period.

We never saw the harvest of the 1955-57 equipment boom. We seemed to fritter away in white collar workers all that we saved in blue collar workers.

So I accept that amendment.

PROFESSOR BURNS: Since Paul and I agree on so much, let me add a further word of agreement. I definitely think we should have had a tax reduction early in 1958. I thought so then, in fact I felt strongly about it, and I still think so. I also think that we should have had a tax reduction in 1960.

I felt unhappy that we didn't get these tax changes. Without crying about what happened or didn't happen, let me merely say that I believe that both economic and political history would have been different if those tax reductions had been made when the economy so badly needed them.

PROFESSOR TURE: It seems to me that Professor Samuelson is saying there are two main lines of development in public economic policy currently: One is the long term, the secular focus of policy, and he says this is a distinguishing concern of "new economics." Let's not debate that point. The second thing that he did was to defend activism in public policy with respect to short-term development.

Let me point out, as a further application of Professor

Burns' historical correction, that the excess profits tax was scheduled to expire on June 30, 1953, and legislation was introduced in the House Ways and Means Committee to accompany that expiration with an acceleration by six months of the automatic reduction in individual income tax rates.

The administration opposed this saying it was excessively expansionary at that point in time. Of course, if we are going to date the onset of the downturn, that's when it occurred. What we ought to conclude from this is that people who were looking at things at the time and offering policy judgments to guide an active fiscal and monetary policy for short-term purposes misread the signs then.

I think from that point on the record is unmistakably clear. They misread it all the time. They did it quite recently. I'll call to your attention that there were some hearings in the late spring of 1957 on the economic and budgetary outlook and the fiscal-policy implications thereof. A large array of very impressive economists and public finance specialists testified to the same thing, before the Joint Economic Committee, that any kind of expansionary public policy at that point would be highly irresponsible and, as I read the National Bureau's record, the recession was then underway.

DR. SAMUELSON: Norman is too kind. He didn't name names. I testified in June of 1957 before the Joint Economic Committee. Irwin Friend was on the panel at the time. I was told later, this was years later, that I had been the most pessimistic of those testifying but far from pessimistic enough. Irwin Friend told me that he did a postmortem on where he went wrong. It was a May-July turning point, as I remember, so we were just at the peak; Friend said that he reproached himself for not having seen it; so he looked to see where he went wrong. He said he went wrong in estimating government expenditures. He said, "I should have listened to George Humphrey. I just didn't believe what he said was going to happen could possibly happen. I went wrong by billions of dollars on what one might call the multiplicand at that time."

PROFESSOR TURE: But Paul, in all fairness, I don't think Irwin should chastise himself so, because that reduction in federal expenditures that resulted from the Secretary of the Treasury stirring up the hornet's nest did not occur until after the recession was well under way. Congress slashed appropriations in the course of the year 1957.

DR. SAMUELSON: No, what Irwin was saying was that he took the subsequent period for which he had forecast and he went through all of the components of his forecasts to see where he had been wrong in that period. It was very heavily in his estimates of the government expenditures.

PROFESSOR BURNS: Since we are doing some chastising, let me just put into the record one historical fact; namely, that in August, 1957, one month after the recession had started according to the National Bureau's chronology, the Federal Reserve Board raised the discount rate.

DR. SAMUELSON: It is worse that that—Mr. Martin made a speech in October speaking about the need to control inflation and when I expressed some surprise to a member of the Federal Reserve System, it was explained to me that Martin had been on a vacation. Perhaps he hadn't been properly briefed. It's on such matters that history rests.

HERBERT STEIN, Committee for Economic Development: I understood Professor Samuelson to have given a somewhat qualified good mark to the restrictive policy of the late 1950s and early 1960s, as having in some way prepared the groundwork for a period of expansion without very much inflation. I wonder whether he foresees the possible necessity of going through such a thing again, if we again revive experience and expectations.

DR. SAMUELSON: I think it would be more accurate to say that I take certain cold comfort from the fact that, even though at the time I didn't espouse it, I must not blind myself to the good that the late 1950s slowdown may have done to our Phillips curve.

I'm not the one to make the recommendation, but I think it might be argued that the optimal policy in a mixed economy like ours might be intermittent periods of letting a certain amount of slack develop, then getting the benefit of this slack in breaking inflationary expectations, and then going on strong.

It was thought that Mr. Lloyd's policy of a pause in

England was stupidity when the Labor government went in. Stop-and-go driving was considered to be the most wasteful kind of driving by analogy with gasoline advertisements. But now Harold Wilson finds himself putting in a price-wage freeze and a pause much greater than the Conservative government had ever toyed with.

I am afraid there may be a time when, in a mixed economy, you need a dose of Paishism, after Frank Paish, who advocates slack in season and out of season. We have plenty of Paishes in this country, so I think I'll let them speak for themselves. There is a limit, after all, for a chap to be the devil's advocate.

PROFESSOR KENDRICKS: Paul, now there is no difference between you and Arthur, if you say that occasional slowdowns are good. I thought you said the difference between the two economists was in the degree of expansionism.

DR. SAMUELSON: No, no, what I'm saying is that I think there is possible merit in that case. But that's not where *I* would draw the balance in summing up.

I want to try activism until it is demonstrated that activism is wrong, but I hope the statute of limitations will keep us from discussing the balance-of-payments aspect of that.

PROFESSOR BRIEFS: The one point that I think failed to be developed is your caveat that in being an activist one has to be concerned about the lags that attend policy measures. It seems to me the essence of your position. I am a little unhappy with the lack of development of this caveat. I wonder if you would explain.

DR. SAMUELSON: There is a problem here. I don't want to gloss over it and that's why I am not prepared to say that there is no need for forecasting. However, I think that in the 1960s by taking the longer cyclical view you could operate on the assumption that the actual swings in the economy were themselves going to be slow and long and, therefore, it wasn't likely that you were going to have to reverse yourself very fast. Hence you didn't have to worry too much about the lags.

I don't want to end on a note of disagreement but I really don't think that the reversals of monetary policy are quite the bad thing that the incautious listener to Professor Burns' first remarks might think. I believe that monetary policy should zigzag. It is the stability of the trend, and leaning against the short-term wind that you want. I think that if we operated a model of the American economy as a Monte Carlo simulation experiment and if you were in fact not to have swings in monetary policy, then you would find that everything else in the economy would get destabilized in some very bad ways. I say this because I don't believe in strict constancy with respect to velocity and other matters, but that's a very long story.

PROFESSOR BURNS: The last thing that I want is to have the last word. But I do want to express appreciation to Professor Samuelson for referring to the incautious listener.

PROFESSOR G. WARREN NUTTER, University of Virginia, Coordinator of the Rational Debate: I wonder if in concluding whether you might have any last word you would like to give. Arthur, would you like to say anything?

PROFESSOR BURNS: I am getting the last word after all and I will try to be brief. Professor Samuelson has indicated that he is more of an expansionist than I am and I would agree. I think he is. He has also indicated that a difference in our value judgments may be responsible for this difference. And once again, I want to say that he is probably right.

I would add, however, that I think I am just as much concerned about the unemployed, about the Negroes, and about the teenagers as is anyone, including Professor Samuelson. But I do not think they are the only ones in the society to consider. There are other people as well whose interest must be taken into account. We must try to concern ourselves with the welfare of the population as a whole.

Secondly, I do not believe that by pushing very hard with an aggressive monetary and fiscal policy, at a time when there are already signs of strain on the nation's resources, one can do more than give momentary help to the unemployed. We have got to think of tomorrow as well as of today.

I have been reading recently Walter Heller's book,

as many of you doubtless have. Walter Heller takes President Eisenhower to task for his concern about our grandchildren. It is perfectly true that in referring to budgetary deficits and the dangers of inflation, President Eisenhower has put a certain emphasis on the morality of shifting burdens to our grandchildren. But all that he ever meant was that what we do today has consequences not only today, but also tomorrow.

Now, one reason why I have been so much concerned about aggressively expansionist policies, not only in recent years but also at other times, is that I have proceeded from a certain judgment, based partly on history and partly on recent trends in economic thinking—namely, that the more militant expansionists will simply not know when to stop. I have thought so over the years and that is why I have deemed it important to issue warnings from time to time. And I have yet to be shown that in this practical judgment I have been entirely wrong.

FOOTNOTES

SECOND LECTURE

[1] Research assistance of Felicity Skidmore is gratefully acknowledged. I have deliberately preserved the informal oral flavor of the exposition.

[2] J. P. Schultz and R. Z. Aliber (eds.), *Guidelines, Informal Controls and the Market Place* (Chicago: University of Chicago Press, 1966), pp. 18 and 19.

[3] P. A. Samuelson, J. R. Coleman, and F. Skidmore (eds), *Readings in Economics* (New York: McGraw-Hill, 1967), pp. 376-77, taken from A. F. Burns, "Wages and Prices by Formula?" *Harvard Business Review*, March-April, 1965, p. 59.

[4] Shultz and Aliber, *op. cit.*, pp. 48-49.

[5] Actually, there is a pitfall here, since the residual must also include taxes; and when we consider more realistic cases, where the prices of raw materials and imports may fluctuate, the non-wage residual is more complicated than would be a mere profit figure.

DISCUSSION

FIRST SESSION

[1] Both Professor Burns and Professor Samuelson have reviewed their remarks throughout the Discussion section. Original transcripts are available at the offices of the American Enterprise Institute.